Objective-C
Pocket Reference

Andrew M. Duncan

O'REILLY®

Beijing · Cambridge · Farnham · Köln · Paris · Sebastopol · Taipei · Tokyo

Objective-C Pocket Reference
by Andrew M. Duncan

Published by O'Reilly & Associates, Inc., 1005 Gravenstein Highway North,
Sebastopol, CA 95472.

O'Reilly & Associates books may be purchased for educational,
business, or sales promotional use. Online editions are also available
for most titles (*safari.oreilly.com*). For more information, contact our
corporate/institutional sales department: (800) 998-9938 or
corporate@oreilly.com.

Editor:	Jonathan Gennick
Production Editor:	Jane Ellin
Cover Designer:	Ellie Volckhausen
Interior Designer:	David Futato

Printing History:

December 2002:   First Edition.

0-596-00423-0
[C]   [4/03]

Contents

Objective-C Pocket Reference

Introduction

The *Objective-C Pocket Reference* is a quick guide to the Objective-C programming language and some of its fundamental support libraries. This reference takes the form of brief explanations interspersed with examples and definitions. If you are experienced with Objective-C, this handbook will supply the definitions and examples you most often need to jog your memory. If you are coming to Objective-C from C++ or Java and prefer to jump right in and write code, this book will give you enough explanation to use the language's features appropriately.

> **NOTE**
>
> You should be familiar with C-style languages in order to read this book. Objective-C uses C syntax. This book focuses only on Objective-C, and assumes that you understand the underlying C code.

This handbook progresses in sequence as much as possible, with later sections building on earlier ones, but some parts are necessarily interrelated. For example, the section on objects needs to refer to classes and vice versa. Both use the terminology of inheritance. Where you see an unfamiliar term used, check the index: it is probably defined elsewhere in the book.

Although Objective-C is (apart from its C base) a small language, the implications of its modest set of extensions are substantial. To use Objective-C effectively, you should follow tested design patterns and make judicious use of libraries. The intent of this handbook is to provide a quick reference to the most commonly used features and idioms of the language. It should be like a fast cache, the first stop for frequently used data.

Because of its size, this handbook can present only an outline of the language, its libraries, and conventional patterns of usage. If you are interested in truly understanding the Objective-C way of thinking, you should also look at some of the texts listed in the "Objective-C Resources" section at the end of this book.

For supplementary information and corrections to this handbook, see our web site at *http://www.oreilly.com/catalog/objectcpr*.

Typographic Conventions

The following typographical conventions are used in this book:

Italic
> New terms, URLs, and filenames

Constant Width
> Code examples and names of classes, fields, variables, and methods

Constant Width Bold
> Words that are reserved in C or Objective-C

Constant Width Italic
> Text in an example that should be replaced by values you supply

Acknowledgments

Many thanks to my attentive editor, Jonathan Gennick, who considers every word. Greg Parker gave valuable feedback about the Objective-C runtime, Mark Bessey about the compiler, and Nicola Pero about archiving. Paul Kmiec asked the tough questions that made me think about how to explain the answers. Thanks also to Jacek Artymiak, Scott Anguish, and Eric Buck for their very thorough technical review of this book.

What Is Objective-C?

Objective-C is an *object-oriented* language: it supports hierarchies of substitutable types, message-passing between objects, and code reuse through inheritance. Objective-C adds these features to the familiar C programming language.

Because Objective-C is an extension of C, many properties of an Objective-C program depend on the underlying C development tools. Among these properties are:

- The size of scalar variables such as integers and floating-point numbers
- Allowed placement of scoped declarations
- Implicit type conversion and promotion
- Storage of string literals
- Preprocessor macro expansion
- Compiler warning levels
- Code optimization
- Include and link search paths

For more information about these topics, consult the documentation for your development platform and tools.

Objective-C differs from C++, another object-oriented extension of C, by deferring decisions until runtime that C++

would make at compile time. Objective-C is distinguished by the following key features:

- Dynamic dispatch
- Dynamic typing
- Dynamic loading

Dynamic Dispatch

Object-oriented languages replace function calls with *messages*. The difference is that the same message may trigger different code at runtime, depending on the type of the message receiver. Objective-C decides dynamically—at runtime—what code will handle a message by searching the receiver's class and parent classes. (The Objective-C runtime caches the search results for better performance.) By contrast, a C++ compiler constructs a dispatch table statically—at compile time.

Because the simple linear search for a receiver used by Objective-C mirrors the way we think about inheritance, it's easy to understand how an Objective-C program works. Dynamic dispatch can handle changes in the inheritance hierarchy at runtime. A dynamic message-sending model is also more natural for distributed objects than a table-based model.

Dynamic Typing

Because message-sending is dynamic, Objective-C lets you send messages to objects whose type has not been declared. The Objective-C environment determines dynamically—at runtime—the class of the message receiver and calls the appropriate code. By comparison, C++ requires the type of the receiver to be declared statically—at compile time—in order to consult dispatch tables.

Static typing allows the compiler to detect some program errors, but type checking is undecidable—that is, no algorithm can infallibly distinguish between programs that have type errors and those that do not. A compiler must either miss some errors or prohibit some safe operations. Of course, in practice compilers follow the latter course, so some programs that would run correctly will not compile. Dynamic typing admits designs whose correctness is not evident to the compiler.

Objective-C lets you use static type checking where you want it, but dynamic typing where you need it. This represents a move away from the question of *What is the receiver's type at compile time?* to *What messages does an object respond to at runtime?* Since programs run only at runtime, this is a more useful perspective.

Dynamic Loading

Because the process of method dispatch is simple and uniform, it's easy to defer until runtime the linking of separately-compiled code modules. Objective-C programs can be factored into components that have minimal interdependency; these components can be loaded as needed by a running program. This makes it easier to deliver code, as well as content, over a network; design applications or systems that are distributed; or write an application that can be extended by third-party plug-ins.

Which Objective-C?

If you are programming in a Unix environment, you probably already have an Objective-C compiler: the *gcc* compiler, which is part of many Unix installations and is available under the terms of the GNU Public License. Because of the wide availability of this compiler for many software and hardware platforms, this handbook documents the features of the language compiled by Version 3.1 of *gcc*.

Apple Computer has also adopted *gcc* as the compiler for its OS X platform, which is based on a Unix variant called

Darwin. Darwin provides its own Objective-C runtime, and a class library called Cocoa. This handbook notes the differences between the Darwin and GNU runtime environments, and documents the root classes supplied by both GNU and Cocoa.

There is also a class library called GNUstep, distributed under the terms of the GNU Lesser (Library) Public License. GNUstep is an outgrowth of the same code that gave rise to Cocoa, and is largely compatible with Cocoa. Discussions in this book of Cocoa features such as the NSObject root class will apply equally to the GNUstep version.

How Do I Get Started?

Here is a minimal Objective-C program. If you can successfully compile and run it, your Objective-C installation is working correctly.

```
#import <objc/Object.h>
int main(int argc, char* argv[ ]) {
  Object* obj = [Object new];
  return 0;
}
```

To build this program from a shell prompt, save it in a file named *myProg.m* and issue the following commands. (Your platform may require a different threading library, which is specified in the last parameter. If you are using an integrated development environment, follow its documentation for building a program.)

```
gcc -c myProg.m
gcc -o myProg myProg.o -lobjc -lpthread
```

When this little program succeeds in compiling, you are ready to start learning the language and writing Objective-C programs.

Elements of the Language

Objective-C extends the C language with the following concepts and constructs:

- Objects (instances of classes)
- Classes
- Inheritance and subtyping
- Fields
- Methods and method calls (or messages)
- Categories
- Protocols
- Declarations (extended from C to include class and protocol types)
- Predefined types, constants, and variables
- Compiler and preprocessor directives

The following sections will describe these aspects of Objective-C.

Objects

Objects are the compound values—data and operations—at the heart of object-oriented programming. They are generalizations of simple structured types found in C and many other languages. Like C structs, objects have components—data fields—that maintain state. For example, a `Book` object might have fields to specify the author and publisher. In addition, objects interact through message passing, which provides an alternative to the function calls of a procedural language.

Objective-C objects have these attributes:

Class
> An object type. An object whose type is `MyClass` is said to be an *instance* of `MyClass`.

Fields

> Data members of an object. An object has its own copies of the fields declared by its class or its ancestor classes.

NOTE

Fields are also referred to as "instance variables." I prefer the term "fields" for several reasons: "instance variables" is redundant since there are no class variables, it is ambiguous since it could mean variables that are instances, just "variables" would be more ambiguous, and "fields" is shorter. (An alternative term is "ivars.")

Methods

> Functions provided by an object. An object responds to methods declared by its class or ancestor classes.

NOTE

A few special objects (class objects) acquire their fields and methods differently. The "Runtime Environment" section describes class objects.

Objective-C objects are implemented so that:

- They exist in dynamically allocated memory.
- They can't be declared on the stack or passed by value to other scopes.
- They are referred to only by pointers.

When someone says of an Objective-C variable: "c is an instance of C", you should understand that to mean that c is a pointer to an object of type C.

Classes

Classes are types in Objective-C. The *interface* of a class specifies the structure of its instances; the *implementation* provides its code. The interface and implementation of a class are separate, usually in different files. Categories add to an existing class without subclassing it; they also have separate interface and implementation. Protocols are pure interface declarations.

Classes declare the following attributes:

Parent class
> The class whose methods and fields will be inherited by the new class being declared.

Class name
> The name of the class being declared.

Fields
> Data members of each instance of the class.

Instance methods
> Functions associated with instances of the class.

Class methods
> Functions associated with the class itself.

Because Objective-C makes calling class methods syntactically identical to calling instance methods, classes themselves behave much like objects. The "Runtime Environment" section discusses class objects.

Declaring an interface

An interface names a class and declares its parent (if any), fields, and methods, without specifying any implementation. (You can't use C++-style inline methods, implemented in the header.) A header file can contain any number of interface declarations, but it is conventional to put each interface in a separate header file. By default, *gcc* expects the filename to end in *.h*.

Following is an example interface declaration. (Note that the line numbers are not part of the source code.)

```
1 #import "Graphic.h"
2
3 @class Point;
4
```

```
 5 @interface Circle : Graphic {
 6   @protected  // or @public or @private
 7      float  radius;
 8      Point* center;
 9 }
10   -(void)scaleBy:(float)factor;
11   +(void)numCircles;
12 @end
```

Line 1. The **#import** directive is like C's **#include** directive, except that the compiler ensures that no file is included more than once. You always need to import the declaration of your class's parent class (if any). You don't need to import any other Objective-C class declarations, but it may be convenient to import some umbrella header files as a matter of routine.

Line 3. You use the **ec@class** declaration when your class's fields, or the return values or parameters of your class's methods, are instances of another class. You can use separate **@class** declarations for distinct classes, or use a single declaration with the class names separated by commas.

A class declaration doesn't need any more information about any other class, so you don't need to import a header unless the header has other declarations (e.g., macros or globals) that your class declaration needs.

Line 5. Specify the name of your class and that of the parent class (if any). The name of your class will be visible to any code that includes the header file. All class names exist in the global namespace, along with global variable names and type names.

Line 6. Access keywords control compile-time checking of access to fields. You can repeat these as often as you want; a field has the access permission specified by the most recent preceding keyword. If there is no preceding keyword, access permission defaults to protected.

In brief, public fields are visible to all subclasses and all external code, protected fields are visible only to subclasses, and private fields are visible only in the class being declared. The "Fields" section gives exact rules.

Line 7. Declare fields in the same manner as you declare structure members in C. Fields can be of any C type, as well as of any class or other type (described in the "Predefined Types, Constants, and Variables" section) added by Objective-C. Fields can have the same name as methods in the same class.

Fields are not shared between instances—that is, Objective-C does not support class variables. But you can get the same effect by declaring ordinary variables as **static** in the implementation file. (See the following "Implementing a class" section for an example.)

Line 8. You incorporate other objects only by pointer, not by value. Objective-C's predefined **id**, Class, and Protocol types are pointer types already.

Line 9. No semicolon after the closing brace.

Line 10. An instance method is marked with a - character. Instance methods operate on instances of the class. Method signatures use Objective-C's infix syntax, discussed later in "Methods."

You don't need to redeclare a method if you are inheriting it. It is conventional to redeclare a method if your class inherits and overrides it. The "Naming collisions" section explains why you should declare a method in all other cases. (But not necessarily in the header file; see "Private methods.") Methods can have the same name as fields of the same class, and instance methods can share names with class methods.

Line 11. A class method is marked with a + character. Class methods perform operations or return information about the class as a whole, and don't pertain to any instance of the class.

Line 12. No semicolon after the **@end** keyword.

Implementing a class

You implement a class by writing the code (i.e., the bodies) for each of the class's methods. A file can contain any number of class implementations, but it is conventional to put each implementation in a separate file. By default, *gcc* expects the filename to end in *.m* (for Objective-C) or *.mm* or *.M* (for Objective-C++). Even if a class has no methods, it must have an empty implementation.

NOTE

If you don't provide a class implementation, the compiler will not emit support code for the class, and the linker will fail.

Here is a simple implementation for the class declared in the previous section:

```
1 #import "Circle.h"
2
3 static int count;
4
5 @implementation Circle
6   // No field section.
7   +(void)numCircles { return count; }
8   -(void)scaleBy:(float)factor { radius *= factor;}
9 @end
```

Line 1. Always import the header file that declares your class. If your code uses other classes (e.g., it sends messages to them or their instances) you need to import the headers of those classes too. There is little point to using an **@class** declaration here—if you use another class in an implementation you will need its interface declaration.

Line 3. This is a pure C declaration, reserving space for a per-class variable. (In this example, it would be used to keep count of the number of objects created. That code is not shown.) It will be visible only in this implementation file.

Line 5. Specify the name of the class you are implementing.

Line 6. You can't add any more fields here, so there is no brace-delimited section corresponding to the one in the interface declaration.

Lines 7, 8. Define methods with the same signature syntax as in the header; follow each method definition with the code, in braces. For more information on writing the code, see the "Methods" section.

Line 9. No semicolon after the **@end** keyword.

Inheritance and Subtyping

Inheritance and subtyping are the fundamental object-oriented features: inheritance lets you declare how one type differs from another, and subtyping lets you substitute one kind of object for another when their types are compatible.

A class's interface may declare that it is based on another class:

```
@interface MyClass : Parent
```

This is described by saying *MyClass* is a *subclass* of *Parent*, and has the following runtime effects:

- *MyClass* responds to any class method that *Parent* responds to.
- Instances of *MyClass* have all the fields that instances of *Parent* have.
- Instances of *MyClass* respond to any instance methods that instances of *Parent* respond to.

These effects are summarized by saying *MyClass* inherits *Parent*'s fields and methods. These properties imply that inheritance is transitive: any subclass of *MyClass* also inherits from *Parent*.

Declaring a class and specifying a parent also has these effects at compile time:

- You can refer to inherited methods and fields.
- You can assign variables declared as *MyClass* to variables declared as *Parent*.

This is described by saying *MyClass* is a *subtype* of *Parent*. Subtyping is also transitive. For example, any subclass of *MyClass* is a subtype of *Parent*.

You can't redeclare fields in a subclass, either identically or with a different type. (Unlike C++, this holds even if the inherited field was declared private.)

A subclass can replace, or *override*, an inherited method with a different version. You do this by providing a new implementation for the method when you write the subclass. At runtime, instances of the subclass will execute the new code in the overriding method instead of the code of the inherited method. By definition, the overriding method has the same name as the inherited one; it must also have the same return and parameter types. (You can't overload methods as in C++.) You don't need to redeclare the overriding method, but it is conventional to do so.

Fields

Fields are data members of objects. Each object gets its own copy of the fields it inherits or declares.

Inside the methods of a class you can refer directly to fields of **self**, either declared in the class or (if they are not private) inherited:

```
@interface Circle : Graphic {
    float radius;   // Protected field.
    // etc.
@end

@implementation Circle
    -(float)diameter {
        return 2 * radius; // No need to say self->radius.
    }
@end
```

If an object other than **self** is statically typed, you can refer to its public fields with the dereference operator:

```
AClass* obj;       // Static typing required.
obj->aField = 7;   // Presuming aField is public.
```

Access modifiers

Access to an object's field depends on four things:

- The field's access permission (public, private, or protected)
- The class of the accessing code
- The class of the object
- The nature of the object: whether it is the receiver (**self**) or another variable (global, local, or method parameter)

There is no notion of read-only members in Objective-C: if you can read a field, you can also write to it.

You declare a field's access permission in its class's interface. Any of three access keywords—**@public**, **@protected**, and **@private**—may appear any number of times in an interface declaration and affects all fields declared after it until the next access keyword. (See the example in the "Classes" section.) If there is no preceding keyword, a field has protected access.

Following are the keywords and their effects on access to an object's fields:

@public
> A public field is visible to all code.

@protected
> If the object is **self**, a protected field is visible.
>
> If the object is not **self**, access depends on its class:
>
> - If the object's class is the same as that of the receiver, the field is visible.
> - If the object inherits from the receiver's class, the field is not visible. (You can get around this by casting the object to the receiver's class.)
> - If the object has any other relation to the receiver's class, the field is not visible.

@private

> If the object is **self**, a private field is visible.
>
> If the object is not **self**:
>
> • If the object's class is the same as that of the receiver, the field is visible.
>
> • In all other cases, the field is not visible.

Methods

Methods are the functions associated with an object, and are used as interfaces for querying or changing the object's state, or for requesting it to perform some action.

Objective-C uses the terms "calling a method" and "sending a message" interchangeably. This is because method dispatch is less like dereferencing a function pointer and more like searching for a recipient and delivering a message. Most of the work of method lookup is done at runtime.

You send messages to objects using Objective-C's bracket syntax. Method names are associated with parameters using an infix syntax borrowed from Smalltalk. Objective-C provides directives for accessing the runtime dispatch mechanism directly.

Declaring a method

You declare a method in an interface or protocol by specifying who handles it (either the class or an instance of the class), its return type, its name, and its parameter types (if any). The name is broken up so that part of it precedes each parameter. The form of a declaration depends on the number of parameters, as described in the following sections.

No parameters

```
-(id)init;
```

This declaration can be broken down as follows:

-

> Indicates an instance method; use a + for class methods.

(id)

> Indicates that the return type is **id**. Specifying a return type is optional; the default return type is **id**.

init

> The method's name.

One parameter

+(**void**)setVersion:(**int**)v;

This declaration can be broken down as follows:

+

> Indicates a class method.

(void)

> Indicates that the return type is **void**.

setVersion:

> The method name. This method name includes a colon, which indicates a parameter to follow.

(int)

> Specifies that the parameter is an **int**. If you omit the parameter type, it defaults to **id**.

v

> The parameter name. You need the name in both declaration and implementation, although it's only used in the implementation.

More than one parameter

-(**id**)perform:(**SEL**)sel with:(**id**)obj;

This declaration can be broken down as follows:

-

> Indicates an instance method.

(id)

> Indicates that the return type is **id**.

`perform:`
> The first part of the method name. This method name has two parts, one preceding each of the parameters. The full method name is `perform:with:`. Methods with more parameters follow the same pattern as shown here. The second, third, etc. parts of a method name don't need any textual characters, but the colons are required.

`(SEL)`
> Specifies that the first parameter has the type **SEL**.

sel
> The name of the first parameter.

`with:`
> The second part of the method name.

`(id)`
> Specifies that the second parameter has the type **id**.

obj
> The name of the second parameter.

A variable number of parameters

`-(id)error:(char*)`*format*`,...;`

This declaration can be broken down as follows:

`-`
> Indicates an instance method.

`(id)`
> Indicates that the return type is **id**.

`error:`
> The entire method name. In this case, the second and subsequent parameters are not prefaced by extensions of the method name.

`(char*)`
> Specifies the type of the first parameter.

format
> The name of the first parameter.

...
> Represents the variable-size parameter list. Ellipses like these can only appear at the end of a method declaration. In the method, access the list using the standard C variable-arguments interface.

Implementing a method

The body of a method appears in the implementation section of a class. The method starts with a declaration, identical to that of the interface section, and is followed by code surrounded by braces. For example:

```
-(void)scaleBy:(float)factor {
  radius *= factor;
}
```

Inside a method body, refer to fields the class declares or inherits with no qualification. Refer to fields of other objects using the dereference (->) operator.

Objective-C defines three special variables inside each method:

self
> The receiver of the method call.

super
> A reference to the inherited version of the method, if there is one.

_cmd
> The selector—an integer that uniquely specifies the method.

The "Predefined Types, Constants, and Variables" section describes these special variables in more detail.

Calling a method

Every method call has a receiver—the object whose method you are calling—and a method name. You enclose a method call in brackets [ ] with the receiver first and the method name following. If the method takes parameters, they follow the corresponding colons in the components of the method name. Separate receiver and name components by spaces. For example:

```
[aCircle initWithCenter:aPoint andRadius:42];
```

If a method takes a variable number of parameters, separate them with commas:

```
[self error:"Expected %d but got %d", i, j];
```

A method call is an expression, so if the method returns a value you can assign it to a variable:

```
int theArea = [aCircle area];
```

Method calls can be nested:

```
Circle* c1 = ... // whatever
Circle* c2 =
  [[Circle alloc] initWithCenter:[c1 center]
                  andRadius:[c1 radius]];
```

Naming collisions

When the compiler encodes a method call, it needs to set up, then and there, room for the parameters and return value (if any). This is a nondynamic aspect of method calls. To encode the call properly, the compiler must know the parameter and return types.

If you leave the type of a receiver unknown (that is, declared as **id**) until runtime, the name of a method may be all the information the compiler has when it compiles the method call. The compiler will encode the method call based on previous uses of the same method:

- If the compiler has not yet seen any methods with the name used, it will assume the return type and parameters are all **id** (a pointer whose size is platform-dependent) and will issue a warning message. If you use variables of type other than **id**, the compiler will convert them according to standard C rules and they may not survive intact.

- If the compiler has seen exactly one method with the same name, it will emit code assuming the return and parameter types match those it saw.

- If the compiler has seen more than one method with the same name, and differing return or parameter types, it will not know how to encode the method call. It will choose one option and issue a warning message. As in the first case, type conversions may play havoc with your data values.

The compiler will not let you declare, in related classes, methods with the same name but different parameter types (no C++-style overloading), but you can do this in unrelated classes. To avoid forcing the compiler to guess your intentions, methods with the same name, even in different classes, should usually have the same signature.

You can relax this restriction if you know the receiver of the call will always be statically typed. But you may not have control over all future use of your method.

Private methods

Because the compiler needs to know parameter types to generate method calls, you should also not omit method declarations in an attempt to make them private. A better way to make a method private is to move the method declaration to its class's implementation file, where it will be visible to the code that uses it but not to any other part of your program.

The following example shows how to use a category (described at greater length in the "Categories" section) to declare a method in an implementation file:

```
1 @interface Circle (PrivateMethods)
2   -(float)top;
3 @end
```

```
4
5 @implementation Circle
6   // Public definitions as before.
7   ...
8   // Now implement the private methods.
9   -(float)top { return [center y] - radius; }
8 @end
```

Line 1. At the beginning of your class's implementation file, declare a category that extends the class.

Line 2. Methods declared here are just as much part of the class as the ones declared in the regular interface, but will be visible only in this file.

Line 5. Your class's implementation, in the usual fashion.

Line 6. Implement the methods declared in the header file. They can call the private methods (as well as other public methods, of course).

Line 8. Implement the private methods. They can call public and private methods.

Accessors

Accessors are methods for setting and returning an object's fields. Objective-C has several conventions for writing accessors:

- To return a variable, provide a method with the same name as the variable. You can do this because methods and fields have separate namespaces.

- To set a variable, provide a method with the same name as the variable that takes the new value as a parameter. For example, given a variable named radius, use radius: (float)r as the signature for your setter method. You can do this because the colon preceding the parameter is part of the methods' name, so radius: the setter will be differently named from the radius the getter.

Here is an example of how to write accessors for a simple field:

```
@implementation Circle
  -(float)radius { return radius; }
  -(void)radius:(float)r { radius = r; }
@end
```

NOTE

Don't use "get" in the name of your accessors. By convention, methods whose names start with "get" take an address into which data will be copied.

If you are using reference counting, there are more design patterns you should follow when writing accessors. These are discussed in the "Reference Counting" section.

Message search paths

When you send an object a message (call one of its methods), the code that actually runs is determined by a search performed at runtime.

The dispatch of the method call proceeds as follows:

1. The runtime system examines the object at the actual time the message is sent and determines the object's class.

2. If that class has an instance method with the same name, the method executes.

3. If the class does not have such a method, the same search takes place in the parent class.

4. The search proceeds up the inheritance tree to the root class. If a method with a matching name is found, that method executes.

5. If there is no matching method but the receiver has a forwarding method, the runtime system calls the forwarding method. (See "Forwarding Messages.") Default forwarding behavior is to exit the program.

---

6. If there are no forwarding methods, the program normally exits with an error. The "Runtime Environment" section describes how to change this.

The "Runtime Environment" section provides more details about method dispatch.

Special receivers

The receiver is the object to which you are sending a message. Its instance methods will be given the first chance to handle the call, followed by the instance methods of its ancestor classes.

Besides the typical case of sending a message to a named receiver, there are several special targets:

self
> Refers to the object that is executing the current method. At runtime, the class of **self** may be the class in which the call to **self** appears, or it may be a subclass.

super
> Refers to the inherited version of the method.
>
> When you use the predefined variable **super** as the receiver, you are sending a message to **self** but instructing the runtime to start method lookup in the parent class of the class in which the send occurs.
>
> This is not the same as starting in the parent class of the receiver—the class of **super** is determined at compile time. If this were done dynamically, the following code would cause an infinite loop:

```
1 @implementation C
2   -(void) f { [super f]; }
3 @end
4
5 // And elsewhere:
6 D* d = [D new];
7 // D inherits from C, does not override f.
8 [d f];  // Executes in C's version.
```

Here, *D* is a subclass of *C* that does not override *f*. The call at line 8 would dispatch to line 2, but the call to **super** would be redirected to the parent class (*C*) of the receiver (*D*)—i.e., back to line 2.

Any class name

Refers to the class object that represents the named class. When you call a class method you are actually sending a message to a class object. (See the "Runtime Environment" section.) If you don't have the class object on hand, this syntax lets you use the class's name as the receiver.

nil

It is not an error to send a message to **nil** (an uninitialized or cleared object). If the message has no return value (**void**), nothing will happen. If the message returns an object pointer, it will return **nil**. If the message returns a scalar value such as an **int** or **float**, it will return zero. If the message returns a **struct**, **union**, or other compound value, its return value is not specified and you should not depend on it. This behavior makes it easier to chain together method calls. For example:

```
id widget = [[[window child] toolbar] widget];
```

If sending a message to **nil** caused a runtime error, you would have to check the result of each message. This property of **nil** should not tempt you to be lax with your runtime checking, but it may suffice to test only the end result of a chain of method calls.

Selectors

Objective-C methods are distinguished by their names, which are the concatenation of the component parts of the method name, including the colon characters. At compile time, each name is matched to a unique integer called the *selector*. The Objective-C type **SEL** represents a selector's type.

When a method call is compiled, it is distilled to its receiver, selector, and parameters. At runtime, the message is dispatched by matching the selector with a list maintained by the receiver's class object.

You can use selectors to make a runtime decision about what method to call—the Objective-C version of function or method pointers.

```
1 SEL mySel = @selector(center);
2 Point* p = [aCircle perform:mySel];
```

Line 1. The compiler knows the mapping from selector names to **SEL**s and will emit code assigning to *mySel* the value corresponding to the method name *center*.

Line 2. Using the selector, you can instruct the receiver to respond to the message as if it had been sent in the usual way. The effect is the same as executing the direct method call:

```
Point* p = [aCircle center];
```

The "Root Classes" section gives more information about the -perform: methods.

Categories

Objective-C provides the category construct for modifying an existing class "in place." This differs from writing a new subclass: with inheritance you can only create a new leaf in the inheritance tree; categories let you modify interior nodes in the tree.

With a category, the full declaration of a class can be spread out over multiple files and compiled at different times. This has several advantages:

- You can partition a class into groups of related methods and keep the groups separate.
- Different programmers can more easily work on different parts of the class.

- For diverse applications, you can provide only those parts of the class that are needed. This gives you finer-grained control over expressing dependencies without having to provide different versions of the class.

- You can add methods to classes from the operating system's library or from third-party sources without having to subclass them.

Declaring a category

Here is an example of declaring a category to add methods to the Circle class:

```
1 #import "Circle.h"
2
3 @interface Circle (Motion)
4    // No field section.
5    -(void)moveRight:(float)dx;
6    -(void)moveUp:(float)dy;
7 @end
```

Line 1. The declaration can be in the same header file as the declaration of the class it modifies, or in a separate file. If it is in a separate header file, you may need to include the header file of the modified class.

Line 3. Declare the name of the class you are modifying and the name of your category. In this example, Circle is the class name, and Motion is the category name. Category names have their own namespace, so a category can have the same name as a class or a protocol.

Line 4. There is no fields section in the category declaration, so you can't use a category to add fields to a class.

Lines 5, 6. Declare methods here as in a class interface.

Line 7. No semicolon after the @end keyword.

You can declare a category in a header or an implementation file. If the declaration is in a header file, its methods are full members of the modified class. Any code can use the new methods with the modified class (and its subclasses). If the declaration is in an implementation file, only code in that file can use the new methods, and their implementation must appear in that file. This is a way of making methods private.

If you declare in your category a method with the same name as one in the modified class, the new method overrides the old one. When such an overriding method sends messages to **super**, they go to the same method in the parent class (just as they would in the overridden version) and not to the overridden method itself. You can't send messages to the overridden version. You should simply avoid using categories to override methods.

If several categories that modify the same class all declare a method with the same name, the results are implementation dependent. In other words, don't do this. The *gcc* compiler does not warn you about this.

You don't have to implement all or even any of the methods you declare in a category. The compiler will warn you if you have an implementation section for your category and omit any methods. If you have no implementation at all for a category, this is called declaring an informal protocol. The "Protocols" section discusses these further.

Implementing a category

You implement the methods of the category in an implementation file, like this:

```
1 #import "Motion.h"
2
3 @implementation Circle (Motion)
4   -(void)moveRight:(float)dx { ... }
5   -(void)moveUp:(float)dy { ... }
5 @end
```

Line 1. You need to include the declaration of the category you are implementing. If the declaration is in the same file as the implementation, you don't need this line.

Line 3. Specify the name of the modified class and the name of your category.

Line 4. Methods take the same form and have the same access to fields as in a regular class implementation.

Line 5. No semicolon after the **@end** keyword.

Protocols

Protocols are lists of method declarations that are not associated with a specific class declaration. Protocols let you express that unrelated classes share a common set of method declarations. (This facility inspired Java's interface construct.) Protocols let you do the following:

- Use static type checking where you want it
- Specify interfaces to other code
- Factor common features of your class hierarchy

Objective-C declarations can specify that an instance must support a protocol, instead of (or in addition to) conforming to a class. (See the "Declarations" section.)

Declaring a protocol

You declare a protocol in a header file like this:

```
1 @protocol AnotherProtocol;
2
3 @protocol Printable <Drawable>
4   -(void)print;
5 @end
```

Line 1. You need the forward protocol declaration if return or parameter types of methods in your protocol use the other protocol.

Protocol names have their own namespace, so a protocol can have the same name as a class or a category.

Line 3. If your protocol extends other protocols, name those in the protocol list. The list is a sequence of protocol names, separated by commas. If the list is empty, you can omit the angle brackets. You don't need to redeclare the methods of the listed protocols. When a class adopts the protocol you are declaring, it must implement all the methods declared in your protocol and all the other protocols in the list. (You can't write partially abstract classes as in C++, with some methods declared but not implemented.)

Line 4. You declare your methods here in the same form as in a class interface.

Line 5. No semicolon after the **@end** keyword.

Adopting a protocol

When you want your class to adopt (implement) one or more protocols, you declare it like this:

```
#import "Printable.h"
@interface Circle : Graphic <Printable>
```

When you want your category to adopt a protocol you declare it like this:

```
#import "Printable.h"
@interface Circle (Motion) <Printable>
```

The list of protocols, inside the angle brackets, consists of names separated by commas. You have to import the header files where the protocols are declared. Don't redeclare the protocol's methods in your interface; just define them in your implementation. You have to define all the methods of the protocol.

When you declare a field or variable, you can specify that it represents an instance whose class conforms to a specific protocol like this:

```
id <Printable> obj;
ClassName <Printable>* obj;
```

For more about this, see the "Declarations" section.

Checking for conformity to a protocol

At runtime, you can check if an object's class conforms to a protocol by using the -conformsTo: (from the root class Object) or +conformsToProtocol: (from NSObject) methods:

```
[obj conformsTo:@protocol(Printable)];
```

Like classes, protocols have special runtime structures associated with them called *protocol objects*. The "Runtime Environment" section describes these.

Informal protocols

You can get some of the functionality of a protocol by declaring but not implementing a category. Such a category is called an *informal protocol*. You can't declare that a class does or does not implement an informal protocol, so you can't use it for static type checking. You can use an informal protocol to specify a group of methods that all subclasses of the modified class *may* implement, but are not obliged to implement. This serves as something less than a full protocol but more than just textual documentation. If you need a protocol, you're better off using a formal protocol.

When a subclass implements an informal protocol, it doesn't refer to the original declaration, but declares in its interface which of the methods it will implement and defines the methods in its implementation in the usual way.

Declarations

You can declare Objective-C objects in many different ways. However, the way in which you declare an object has no effect on that object's runtime behavior. Rather, the way that you declare an object controls how the compiler checks your program for type safety.

Dynamic typing

Use the **id** type to declare a pointer to an unspecified kind of object. This is called *dynamic typing*. For example:

```
id obj;
```

With this declaration, *obj* can be a pointer to an object of any type. An **id** has the following compile-time properties:

- You can send any kind of message to an **id**. (The compiler will warn you if the method name is unknown or ambiguous; see the "Naming collisions" section.) If at runtime the object does not have an appropriate method or delegate (see "Forwarding Messages"), a runtime error will occur (see "Runtime Errors").
- You can assign any other object to an **id**.
- You can assign an **id** to any object. The compiler will not remind you that this can be dangerous. Using an **id** in this way means you assume the risk of assigning an object to an incompatible variable.

Static typing

In Objective-C, any deviation from fully dynamic typing is called *static typing*. With static typing you instruct the compiler about the types of values you intend variables to have. All static typing is done within the inheritance relation: where a variable's class or protocol is declared, a value from a descendant class or protocol is always acceptable.

You can use static typing in three ways, shown in the following examples:

MyClass* obj
> Declares *obj* to be an instance of *MyClass* or one of its descendants. This is called static typing. Declaring *obj* this way has the following compile-time effects:
> - You can assign *obj* to any variable of type **id**.
> - You can assign any variable of type **id** to *obj*.

- You can assign *obj* to any variable whose declared type is *MyClass* or one of its ancestors.

- You can assign to *obj* any variable whose declared type is *MyClass* or one of its descendants.

- The compiler will warn you if you assign *obj* or assign to it in a way not covered in the previous cases. A cast will quiet the compiler but will not prevent an incompatible assignment at runtime.

- You can send to *obj* any message that *MyClass* or one of its parent classes declares.

id *<ProtocolList> obj*

Does not constrain the class of *obj*, but declares that it conforms to the specified protocols. The protocol list consists of protocol names separated by commas. This declaration has the following compile-time effects:

- You can assign *obj* to an object that does not conform to the protocol.

- Assigning *obj* an object that is not declared to conform will trigger a compiler warning.

- Sending to *obj* a message not included in the protocol will trigger a compiler warning.

MyClass <ProtocolList>* obj

Declares that *obj* is an instance of *MyClass* or one of its descendants, and that it conforms to the listed protocols. The compile-time effects of this declaration are the combination of the effects of the preceding two styles of declaration.

NOTE

Due to a compiler bug, *gcc* does not always correctly use the declared protocol for type checking.

Type qualifiers

Type qualifiers go before a C or Objective-C type in a method declaration, and modify that type. Supported qualifiers are:

in	oneway
out	bycopy
inout	byref

These qualifiers can only be used in formal protocols and implementations, not in class or category declarations. They specify how parameters are to be passed when you are using remote messaging. Type qualifiers can be combined, although not all combinations make sense. They are discussed at greater length in the "Remote Messaging" section.

Predefined Types, Constants, and Variables

Objective-C adds the special type **id**, which is generic like a **void*** in C++, but which does not preclude you from sending messages. In addition, the Objective-C environment provides some C types, constants, and variables to support object-oriented programming.

Types

Along with class types that you define, Objective-C introduces these built-in types you can use when declaring variables:

id

> A generic Objective-C object pointer type. You can send any message to the variables of this type without compiler warnings. (See the "Declarations" section.) At runtime the receiver may handle the message, delegate it, or explicitly ignore it. If it does none of these, a runtime exception occurs. (See the "Runtime Errors" section.) Unspecified method return or parameter types default to **id**.

The name **id** is a C typedef for a pointer to a structure with one member: a field that points to a class object. The "Runtime Environment" section discusses this at greater length.

Class

A pure C type: a pointer to an Objective-C class structure. The runtime system contains a structure for each Objective-C class in your program's code. Calling the -class method of any object returns a value of this type.

MetaClass

Provided in the GNU runtime but not in Darwin, this is identical to Class. It's used for clarity when operating with metaclass objects.

Protocol

An Objective-C class. The runtime system contains an instance for each Objective-C protocol that is either adopted by a class in your program's code or referred to in an **@protocol** declaration directive. You can construct a Protocol instance from its name using the **@protocol** directive with a parameter.

BOOL

A logical type whose variables have two possible values: **YES** and **NO**. The name **BOOL** is a typedef for the C type **char**.

SEL

A unique specifier for a method selector. Often implemented as a pointer to the method's name, but you should treat it as an opaque handle. You can construct a selector from a method name using the **@selector** directive.

IMP

A pointer to the implementation of a method that returns an **id**. More precisely, an **IMP** is defined this way:

```
typedef id (*IMP)(id, SEL, ...)
```

The first two parameters are the receiver and selector values that are passed to any method; the remaining variable-length argument list holds the method's visible parameters.

You can construct an **IMP** from a message selector using methods of the root classes Object or NSObject. Calling a method through its **IMP** is considerably faster than using regular dispatch, but may not work correctly if the method does not return an **id**. The section "Optimizing Method Calls" gives an example.

Constants

The following constants are all defined as preprocessor symbols:

nil

A value describing an uninitialized or invalid **id**. Defined to be zero.

Nil

A value describing an uninitialized or invalid Class variable. Defined to be zero.

YES

A value of **BOOL** type, describing a true state. Defined to be one.

NO

A value of **BOOL** type, describing a false state. Defined to be zero.

Variables

These are special variables, set up for you by the Objective-C runtime:

self

Inside an instance method, this variable refers to the receiver of the message that invoked the method.

super

> Not really a variable, but it looks enough like one to be
> included in this list. Inside a method, if you send a mes-
> sage to **super**, method dispatch will start looking in the
> parent class of the method's class. That is, **super** repre-
> sents the static parent, not the parent at runtime.

_cmd

> A variable of type **SEL**, available inside any Objective-C
> method, and describing the selector of the method.

isa

> This is a protected field of all Objective-C objects. You
> do have access to it, although it's better to get it from the
> class method:

```
Class C = obj->isa;     // Discouraged.
Class C = [obj class];  // Better.
```

> isa points to the class object representing the object's
> class.

Compiler and Preprocessor Directives

Compiler and preprocessor directives are special terms in
your program that tell the compiler to perform some Objective-C–specific action. All compiler directives start with the
character @, and preprocessor directives start with #.

Class Declarations and Definitions

The following compiler directives are used to begin or con-
clude the declaration and definition of Objective-C classes,
categories, and protocols:

@interface

> Begins the declaration of a class's or category's fields and
> methods.

@protocol
>   Begins the declaration of a protocol's methods.

@implementation
>   Begins the definition of a class's methods.

@end
>   Ends the declaration or definition of a class's, category's, or protocol's methods.

The use of these compiler directives is described in detail under "Elements of the Language," and especially in the sub-sections "Classes," "Categories," and "Protocols."

Forward Declarations

The following compiler directives generate forward declarations, informing the compiler that a type exists:

@class *ClassName*
>   Forward declaration of a class.

@protocol *ProtocolName*
>   Forward declaration of a protocol.

Use forward declarations when an interface uses variables (fields or method parameters or return types) of a given type. Rather than import the header file for that type, you can simply forward reference it. For example:

```
@class Point;
@interface Circle : Graphic {
  Point* center;
  // etc.
}
@end
```

This is sufficient because the declaration of *Circle* does not use any details of *Point*. You could import the header for *Point*, but this makes any other class that imports *Circle.h* appear dependent also on *Point.h*, and can cause unnecessary (and slow) recompiling in large projects.

Expanding Directives

Expanding complier directives look like functions, but they are really instructions to the compiler, which expands them as described in the following list:

@encode(*typeName*)

Takes a type specification and evaluates to the C string used by the runtime to succinctly describe that type.

@defs(*className*)

Takes the name of an Objective-C class and evaluates to a sequence of type declarations that duplicate the field declarations of the class. This directive can appear only in a C structure declaration.

@protocol(*ProtocolName*)

Evaluates to a pointer to an instance of the Protocol class. You need this because you can't get a protocol class instance by using the protocol name directly, as you can with a class object.

@selector(*MethodName*)

Evaluates to a **SEL** representing the specified method.

@*"string"*

A shorthand for creating a string literal that's an instance of a user-defined string class. Use this when you need a string object constant.

The directives **@encode**, **@defs**, and @*"string"* deserve some additional explanation.

Using @encode

The following example shows how **@encode** can be used to get the string that the Objective-C runtime uses to describe a type:

```
char* itype = @encode(int);
```

The result of this statement will be to define *itype* as the one-character string "i", which is the runtime representation of an **int** type.

The **@encode** directive can take any C or Objective-C type. The runtime uses the mapping between types and strings to encode the signatures of methods and associate them with selectors. You can use **@encode** to implement your own object storage and retrieval, or other tasks that need to describe the types of values.

Table 1 shows the results of applying **@encode** to C and Objective-C types.

Table 1. Types and their encodings

Type	@encode(type)
char	c
int	i
short	s
long	l
long long	q
unsigned char	C
unsigned int	I
unsigned short	S
unsigned long	L
unsigned long long	Q
float	f
double	d
void	v
char*	*
An object pointer	@
Class	#
SEL	:
An array of *N* elements of *type*	[Ntype]

Table 1. Types and their encodings (continued)

Type	@encode(type)
A structure called name with elements $t_1, t_2,$ etc.	{name=t_1t_2...}
A union	(type,...)
A bit field of size N	bN
A pointer to type	^type
Unknown type	?

The runtime system also uses encodings for type qualifiers, shown in Table 2, and you may encounter them in its representation of method signatures. However, you can't get those encodings with the **@encode** directive.

Table 2. Type qualifiers and their encodings

Qualifier	@encode(qualifier)
const	r
in	n
inout	N
out	o
bycopy	O
byref	R
oneway	V

Using @defs

The following example shows how **@defs** can be used to create a C structure with fields that match the fields in a class. In this example, both the order and type of the fields of *MyStruct* will match those in *MyClass*:

```
@interface MyClass : Object {
   int i;
}
@end
```

```
typedef struct {
  @defs(MyClass)
} MyStruct;
```

The typedef in this example is seen by the compiler as:

```
typedef struct {
  id isa;
  int i;
} MyStruct;
```

Having a structure that corresponds to a class lets you bypass the normal access restrictions on an Objective-C instance. In the following example, an instance of *MyClass* is cast to an instance of *MyStruct*. Once that's done, the protected field *i* can be accessed with impunity:

```
MyClass* c = [MyClass new];
MyStruct* s = (MyStruct*)c;
s->i = 42;
```

Obviously this is a facility you should use with restraint.

Using @"string"

The @"*string*" directive creates the Objective-C version of a string literal: one that you can pass to a method expecting a string object, or use to initialize or compare with another string object.

When you create a string with @"*string*", you get an instance of a class defined by the compiler option -fconstant-string-class. The instance is static: its contents are stored in your program's file, and the instance is created at runtime and kept around for the duration of program execution. You can't change its value, because it appears as an expression in your program, not as a variable

In the GNU runtime, the default string class is NXConstantString; for Darwin it is the Cocoa class NSConstantString.

Preprocessor Symbols

Objective-C adds one preprocessor directive and defines one symbol to the preprocessor before compiling:

#import *fileName*
> Using **#import** has the same effect as the C directive **#include**, but will only include the file once.

__OBJC__
> When *gcc* is compiling an Objective-C file, it defines this symbol for the preprocessor. If your code must compile as plain C as well as Objective-C, you can test to see if this symbol is defined:
>
> ```
> #ifdef __OBJC__
>     // Objective-C code here
> #endif
> ```

Compiler Flags

Compiler flags are options you give to *gcc* when it compiles a file or set of files. You may provide these directly on the command line, or your development tools may generate them when they invoke *gcc*. This section describes just the flags that are specific to Objective-C.

-fconstant-string-class=*ClassName*
> Tells the compiler to create an instance of *ClassName* for each string literal expressed with the @"*string*" directive. For the GNU runtime, the default class is NXConstantString; for Cocoa it is NSConstantString.

-fgnu-runtime
> Generate code for linking with the standard GNU Objective-C runtime. This is the default option for most *gcc* installations.

-fnext-runtime
> Generate code for linking with the NeXT runtime. This is the default option for Darwin.

-gen-decls
> Write all interface declarations the compiler sees to a file named *sourcename.decl*.

-Wno-protocol
> Do not warn if methods required by a protocol are not implemented in the class adopting it.

-Wselector
> Warn if there are methods with the same name but different signatures.

Remote Messaging

Objective-C's method call model lends itself well to distributed systems, where sending messages is the fundamental unit of interaction. The key difference in distributed systems is that objects may exist in different address spaces, and so cannot call each other directly.

Objects that want to receive messages from other processes must specify those messages in a formal protocol. Objective-C provides special keywords to use when writing such a formal protocol that qualify the kind of sharing you will need for that protocol's message parameters.

You use the keywords to modify (or qualify) the type of a method's parameter or return value. For example, the keywords out and in modify the parameters in the following declaration:

```
-(void)getData:(out Data*)data
    forIndex:(in int)index;
```

The signature of this method says that *index* is only passed in and changes to it don't need to be returned, but the method will modify the value of *data*.

You can't use these keywords in class or category declarations. However, if your class or category adopts a protocol that uses a remote messaging keyword, you can repeat the keyword in the method signature of the implementation.

The remote messaging keywords can be grouped into three categories: those for pointer parameters, those for return values, and those for object qualifiers.

Pointer Parameter Qualifiers

This section discusses qualifiers that generally apply to pointer arguments. They tell the compiler how to handle copying values between address spaces so that the pointers can be dereferenced in both spaces and see the same value. The pointer parameter qualifiers are as follows:

in

> You will reading directly from the parameter, or will dereference the parameter to read a value but not to write one. This qualifier can be used for non-pointers.

out

> You will dereference the parameter to write a value but not to read one. This qualifier applies only to pointers.

inout

> You will dereference the parameter both to read and write a value. This qualifier applies only to pointers.

If you do not specify a qualifier, the compiler will assume a parameter is **inout**.

Certain types have special behavior with pointer qualifiers. For example, when you declare a C-style string with type **char***, the runtime system treats this as a value type (with value equal to the character string pointed to) and not a pointer, and ships the entire string across between method calls. If you want to pass a string by reference, you need to add another asterisk to its declaration in the parameter list for the method receiving the string.

The runtime treats Objective-C objects the same way. If you want assignments to the parameter to have an effect back in the calling code, you need to add an asterisk in the parameter declaration. Note that passing objects by reference in this sense is not the same as using the **byref** qualifier (described later in "Object Qualifiers").

Return Value Qualifiers

Qualifying a method's return type with **oneway** means the method executes asynchronously—that is, its caller can continue execution without waiting for a response. Use **oneway** only in conjunction with methods with **void** return type.

Object Qualifiers

Object qualifiers modify types that describe instances of classes, either dynamically typed as **id** or statically with a class name, and specify whether the runtime needs to provide for interprocess method calls. The types modified can be either parameters or return types.

bycopy
> This parameter or returned object should be copied between address spaces (rather than setting up a proxy for inter-process method calls). The receiving code must know about the class of the object it gets.

byref
> The opposite of **bycopy**. This parameter or returned object should be exchanged by reference, and a proxy should be set up for handling method calls.

The default behavior is specified in the code for the class itself. In most cases the default is **byref**.

Object Lifecycle

Your classes will have methods that distinguish them from other classes and make them useful, but all classes must implement methods that manage their lifecycle—allocation, initialization, copying, and deletion. In addition, you will use

---

library classes that come supplied with these methods, which you need to use in a consistent way. This section describes the design patterns that Objective-C programmers use and that library classes support.

The root classes `Object` and `NSObject` provide the following methods for managing the lifecycles of objects:

```
+initialize
+alloc
+new
-init
-copy
-dealloc
```

In addition, `Object` also provides these methods:

```
-shallowCopy
-deepCopy
-deepen
-free
```

In addition to these methods, many classes will provide more methods for initializing newly allocated objects.

The "Root Classes" section describes how these methods behave for the root classes; this section gives you guidelines on how to actually use the methods in your programs.

In managing the lifecycle of an object, you are faced with two issues: how to call these methods and how to write them for your own classes. Each of the following sections will first discuss how to call the methods, and then how to write them.

Creating an Object

Objective-C separates object creation into two steps: allocating memory and initializing fields. Allocation returns a pointer to cleared memory where the object will be stored. Initializing an object means setting its fields to some values, either default or specified. These operations serve distinct purposes, are performed by different objects (allocation by a class, and initialization by an instance), and you write and call each of them explicitly.

Calling creation methods

To create an object, you first ask its class to allocate memory, and then you initialize the instance:

```
1 Circle* c = [Circle alloc];
2 c = [c init];
```

Line 1. In Objective-C you call a class method to return a pointer to memory for a new object. It is conventional to call this method +alloc. Both Object and NSObject supply an +alloc method. The object you get from +alloc will have all its fields set to zero.

Line 2. An *initializer* is an instance method that sets the fields of a newly allocated object. Every object responds to the -init message, which it inherits from the root class. The root class version does nothing, but leaves the object in its pristine just-allocated state. Descendants may override -init to provide a default initialization.

An initializer returns the initialized object, but that object may be different from the receiver of the initialization message. For example, an initializer may fail and return **nil**, or substitute a proxy or other special object for the one passed in. For this reason it is not safe to call an initializer as a void method:

```
[c init];   // Discards return value.
```

In this example, any return value is discarded. If -init returns an object different from the receiver, this code will lose that object and the receiver will not be correctly initialized. To avoid this problem, chain the calls to allocate and initialize your objects, or use the new method, which does this for you (but only for the bare-bones -init method). Both of the following lines allocate and initialize an instance of *Circle*:

```
Circle* c1 = [[Circle alloc] init];
Circle* c2 = [Circle new];  // Same effect.
```

Many classes will supply more initialization methods; it is conventional for their names to start with init. These methods may take additional parameters to guide the setting up of the receiver's state. For example:

```
Circle* c = [[Circle alloc] initWithRadius:3];
```

Writing creation methods

Your code should maintain the separation of allocation and initialization. You must also implement the chaining of initializers that ensures that objects are initialized first as instances of their root class, and successively as instances of more derived classes.

To coordinate these steps you are obliged to manage details of object creation that other languages automate. The advantage is that you can more easily understand the behavior of your program by direct inspection.

Your class should always inherit or provide a class method for returning a pointer to cleared memory where the object will be stored. You shouldn't override this method in subclasses. In addition to reserving memory, +alloc needs to set up the internal structure of an object before it is initialized. This makes writing a root class difficult, and your class should usually inherit its allocator from a root class provided by your development environment. Both Object and NSObject supply an +alloc method. If you need to write your own root class, look at *Object.m* to see how this is done.

When an object is initialized, it should become a valid, consistent instance of its class. For this to happen, all Objective-C classes need to cooperate to ensure several things:

- All the ancestors of a class must initialize an object before the class itself does.
- Ancestor initialization must proceed in order from the root class to the most-derived class.

- All ancestor initialization calls should be usable on a class's instance. (The difficulty here is guaranteeing that the class's own initialization will not be skipped.)

Objective-C programmers have adopted the following design patterns to ensure these conditions are always met:

- Your class may have several initialization methods; it is conventional to name those methods starting with init.
- The most specialized initializer (usually the one with the most parameters) is called the *designated initializer* and has a special role: all your class's other initializers should call it.
- Your class should override the parent class's designated initializer.
- Your designated initializer should call the parent class's designated initializer.

The rationale for these guidelines is presented in the next section in the context of a concrete example.

Sample code for initialization

The following code illustrates the design pattern you should follow to ensure correct initialization of your objects. In the example, you are writing the subclass *MyClass*. We assume the parent class follows the same rules we illustrate in the subclass.

```
1 @interface Parent : Object {
2    int i;
3 }
4    -(id)init;
5    -(id)initWithI:(int)val;
6 @end
7
8 @interface MyClass : Parent {
9    int j;
10 }
11    -(id)initWithI:(int)iVal;
12    -(id)initWithI:(int)iVal andJ:(int)jVal;
13 @end
```

```
14
15  @implementation MyClass
16    -(id)initWithI:(int)iVal {
17      return [self initWithI:iVal andJ:42];
18    }
19    -(id)initWithI:(int)iVal andJ:(int)jVal {
20      if (self = [super initWithI:iVal]) {
21        j = jVal;
22      }
23      return self;
24    }
25  @end
```

Line 4. All initializers return **id**. This class has a simple -init method, taking no parameters. It calls (funnels to) -initWithI: passing in a default value.

Line 5. *Parent* provides another initializer, initWithI:, which lets you specify the value of the field *i*. This is the designated initializer.

Line 11. *MyClass* overrides (covers) its parent's designated initializer. Always do this in your classes.

NOTE

If you don't cover a parent's designated initializer, code such as:

```
MyClass* obj =
    [[MyClass alloc] initWithI:42];
```

will go straight to the parent class's initializer and leave *j* undefined.

You must cover all the parent class's initializers; if the parent class funnels all its initializers through the designated initializer (as we are assuming here), overriding it will cover them all. Full coverage ensures that your subclass instances will be substitutable for parent class instances.

Line 12. Provide specialized initializers for your class's specific new features. This method is the designated initializer for *MyClass*.

Line 17. All your class's other initializers should call (funnel to) your class's designated initializer. Funneling lets future subclasses cover all your initializers by just overriding the designated initializer. Pass in to your designated initializer some desired default value for parameters not specified in the simpler initializer.

Line 20. Your designated initializer should first call (chain to) the parent's designated initializer. Calling the parent initializer ensures that all the parent classes will get their chance to initialize the object.

> **NOTE**
>
> Calling the parent designated initializer avoids a circular call path: if instead you called -init here, its (presumed) call to -initWithI: would be dispatched to your new version, and from there back to this method.

You first assign the result of the chaining call to **self**, in case the call returns an object different from the receiver. Then test for **nil** (the **if** statement does this) in case the parent class failed to initialize the object.

Line 21. Your designated initializer performs class-specific work.

Line 23. If your initializer fails, it should return **nil**. The way this example is written, that happens automatically. If your initializer performs more complicated steps, you may have to ensure this explicitly.

Initializing classes

The runtime system will call a class's +initialize class method some time before that class or any of its descendant classes is used. Each class will receive the initialize message before any of its subclasses. If you have some set-up code for the class as a whole (apart from its instances) you should implement this method.

If your class implements +initialize but it has a subclass that does not, the call to initialize the subclass will be handled by your class—that is, your class will receive the message more than once. For this reason, you should guard against multiple calls in your method:

```
+(id)initialize {
  static BOOL done = NO;
  if (!done) {
    // Your initialization here.
    done = YES;
  }
  return self;
}
```

This example is for descendants of Object; the NSObject version of +initialize returns **void** instead of returning an **id**.

Copying an Object

When an object has only value types for fields (apart from the isa pointer), making a copy is a simple matter of duplicating all the fields in a new memory location. When some of the fields are pointers, there are two types of copy that you can make:

- A *shallow copy* duplicates the pointers by value, so the new object refers to the same objects as did the original one.
- A *deep copy* duplicates the objects pointed to, and continues this process, traversing all the pointers of duplicated objects.

The root classes provide a basic framework of copy methods, but your classes will have to override them to get proper deep copying.

Calling copy methods

The copy methods of Object all return a shallow copy of the receiver. For Object itself, the distinction between deep and shallow is meaningless, since the only pointer it has is the isa pointer, which is supposed to be shared between all instances. In descendant classes that properly override the methods, their behavior will be as follows:

-(**id**)copy
> Returns a deep copy of the receiver.

-(**id**)shallowCopy
> Returns a shallow copy of the receiver.

-(**id**)deepen
> Modifies the receiver, replacing all of its non-value fields with deep copies.

-(**id**)deepCopy
> Returns a deep copy of the receiver.

The NSObject class provides only the -copy method, and it simply calls the unimplemented method -copyWithZone:. You need to consult a class's documentation to know if it supports copying. The next section describes how to implement this method yourself to support copying in your classes.

When you get a copy of an object in Cocoa, it has already been retained for you and you will have to call release on it when you are done with it. The "Memory Management" section explains more about retaining and releasing objects.

Writing copy methods

To implement copying for subclasses of Object, you only need to override the -deepen method to recursively traverse the receiver's pointers and replace them with pointers to newly allocated objects identical to the originals.

Cocoa doesn't implement any copying methods for you; it just declares two copying protocols. These protocols don't distinguish between shallow and deep copies: it is up to your classes to decide (and document) what kind of copies they will return. The protocols do distinguish between mutable and immutable copies. A mutable object is one whose values can change; an immutable one must stay constant after it is created. The protocols are:

NSCopying
> Declares the method -copyWithZone:. Adopt this protocol and implement the method to return a copy of the receiver. You must at least adopt this protocol to support copying. If you also adopt NSMutableCopying, -copyWithZone: should return an immutable copy.

NSMutableCopying
> Declares the method -mutableCopyWithZone:. If your class distinguishes between mutable and immutable values, adopt this protocol and implement the method to return a mutable copy of the receiver.

Each method takes as a parameter a pointer to an NSZone, which isn't a class but an opaque type. Normally you will not look any deeper into the zone parameter, but pass it along to an inherited copy method like -allocWithZone: or a Cocoa runtime function like NSZoneAlloc(). See the Cocoa documentation for information on how to use the runtime functions for allocating memory.

Since NSObject does not implement either protocol, you must adopt and implement the protocols if you want your objects to support copying. Your class will inherit from NSObject, whose methods -copy and -mutableCopy call the respective protocol methods (with **nil** parameters) so you can use those simpler methods to make copies of your class's instances.

If the distinction between mutable and immutable doesn't matter for your class (all instances are mutable or all are immutable), just adopt NSCopying. If instances may be one or the other kind, adopt both NSCopying and NSMutableCopying, using the first for returning immutable copies and the second for mutable ones.

If your class doesn't inherit any -copyWithZone: method, implement it using +allocWithZone: and an initialization method. For example:

```
-(id)copyWithZone:(NSZone*)zone {
  return [[self class] allocWithZone:zone] init];
}
```

In this example, you evaluate [self class] to get the receiver of the allocation message. Don't use the name of your class here. If you do, descendants won't be able to inherit this method because the kind of object it creates will be hard-wired.

If your class inherits a -copyWithZone: method, you might not need to change it, for example if your class doesn't add any fields. If you do override this method, it should first call the same method on **super** before doing any further work. For example:

```
-(id)copyWithZone:(NSZone*)zone {
  MyClass* copy = [super copyWithZone:zone];
  // Further class-specific setup of copy.
  return copy;
}
```

If the inherited method returns a shallow copy, the copy will have two properties you will have to correct:

- Its reference count will be identical to your own, and you will have to set the count to 1.
- If it has any pointers to reference-counted objects, the counts of those objects will not be properly incremented by 1 to reflect their additional owner. You should set these fields to **nil** and then initialize them using the appropriate setter method.

WARNING

If you don't set a reference to **nil** first, the setter method may call -release on the referent, leaving its reference count permanently off by one.

If objects of your class are immutable, or there is only one instance that is shared, just call -retain on the receiver and return it to the caller. For example:

```
-(id)copyWithZone:(NSZone*)zone {
  return [self retain];
}
```

Deallocating an Object

The deallocation method of a class complements both the allocation and initializers, undoing the work they did.

Calling deallocation methods

The Object class provides a -free method. Calling this method releases the memory directly associated with the object. Memory directly associated with an object includes the space taken up by that object's fields. If a field is a pointer to an object or other structure, only the pointer will be freed. Subclasses should override this method to adapt its behavior to free additional resources held by the receiver.

The NSObject class provides an analogous method called -dealloc. It has the same behavior as -free, but you don't normally call -dealloc yourself on an object. Instead you use the reference counting methods for memory management, provided by Cocoa. When an object's reference count goes to zero, -dealloc is automatically called. See the "Memory Management" section for information about using reference counting.

Writing deallocation methods

If you're using the Object class, your code will call the -free methods directly. In Cocoa, the runtime will send a -dealloc message to your object when its memory is being freed via the -release message. In either case you use the same approach to writing the deallocators.

Your class's deallocator should first release all resources that it has acquired, *then* call its parent class's deallocator method:

```
-(id)free {
  // Release held resources.
  [super free];  // Tail call.
}
```

Notice that this chaining order is reverse that of initializing: a tail call instead of a head call.

NOTE

Descendants of NSObject will use -release instead of -free.

Resources to be released include Objective-C objects held by reference (call -free or -release on these) and external shared entities like network sockets. The root class deallocator releases the memory of the object (i.e., its fields) itself.

Runtime Errors

Runtime errors include program errors like unhandled method calls or messages sent to released objects, and hardware errors like division by zero. The Object root class provides simple error-handling capability; the Cocoa framework implements exception raising and handling.

Object Error Handling

When an error occurs, the runtime sets in motion the following sequence of events:

1. The runtime calls the -error: method on the object whose method generated the error. You can override this method to customize error handling for a particular class.

---

2. The -error: method prepares information about the receiver and passes it to the runtime C function objc_verror( ).

3. The objc_verror( ) function calls the runtime error handler function if there is one; otherwise it writes an error message to stderr. You can provide a handler function to customize error handling for all classes.

4. If the error handler exists (because you've provided one) and it returns **YES**, execution continues; otherwise the program calls the C function abort( ) and exits.

The GNU runtime provides a function to set your own error handler function:

```
objc_error_handler objc_set_error_handler(objc_error_
handler f)
```

Calling this function sets a new error handler and returns the previous one. The default error handler is a **NULL** pointer. The required signature of an error handler is declared (in *objc-api.h*) as:

```
typedef BOOL (*objc_error_handler)
  (id receiver,
   int errCode,
   const char* format,
   va_list args);
```

Here are descriptions of the parameters your error handler will get:

receiver
> The object in whose method the error occurred.

errCode
> One of a set of integers declared in the header file *objc-api.h* along with objc_error_handler.

format
> A printf-style C string, for printing an error message.

args
> A variable-length list of values for the format string. You can print the error message using the format and argument list and the C function vprintf( ).

Use the first two parameters to decide how to handle the error, and the second two to print a message.

Exceptions in Cocoa

The Cocoa framework contains an NSObject class that provides similar error-handling to the GNU Object. However, Cocoa also provides a more elaborate exception mechanism for handling errors.

An exception is a runtime event that diverts a program from its normal flow of control. In the extreme case, the program will exit immediately. More generally, control may jump across several stack frames, bypassing permanently the remaining code in nested method calls. (Cocoa uses the C setjmp( ) and longjmp( ) calls to implement this.) The Objective-C runtime or your code may generate ("raise") exceptions to signal an event that must be handled in a special way.

Cocoa's exception handling partitions your code into three types:

Try blocks
> A block of code whose exceptions (if raised) will be sent to the immediately following handler section. Always precedes a handler. (The term "try" is borrowed from C++, even though Objective-C doesn't use it as a keyword.)

Handlers
> A block of code executed if an exception is raised. A handler always follows a try block.

Ordinary code
> Any code that is not in a try block or handler.

These kinds of code play the following roles when an exception is raised:

- If execution is in a try block, control jumps to the subsequent handler.
- If execution is in ordinary code (or a handler), the following sequence occurs:
    1. One stack frame is popped from the runtime call stack.
    2. Control returns immediately to the routine that called the just-exited routine.

This process repeats from the first bullet point until either control is inside a handler or the entire call stack is popped.

The result is that a handler will handle exceptions raised directly in its preceding during block, and may handle those generated indirectly (through any level of routine calls), if there are no handlers closer to the source of the exception. If there are no explicit handlers in the current call chain, the uncaught exception handler will be called.

Keywords for handling exceptions

The Cocoa framework provides some definitions, variables, and functions to simplify exception creation, propagation, and handling:

NS_DURING

Starts a try block: a region of code that may generate exceptions. You don't have to test the result of each operation to see if an exception occurred: if one does, control will jump to the handling section.

NS_HANDLER

Starts an exception handling section that corresponds to the preceding try block. In this section, the variable localException will exist and be set to the exception raised.

NS_ENDHANDLER
> Ends the exception handling section.

NS_VOIDRETURN
> Exits a method without returning a value. Use this macro when you need to exit a method from within a try block. Do not use the **return** keyword inside of a try block.

NS_VALUERETURN(*value*)
> The same as **NS_VOIDRETURN**, but used to return a value.

NOTE

If you leave the method using **return**, the exception mechanism will lose track of the call stack. If later code raises an exception, your program will probably crash.

---

localException
> Defined in the handler with the value of the exception that was raised to get there.

NSUncaughtExceptionHandler
> A C typedef for a function that takes an NSException* and returns **void**. The return or parameter type for the following two functions:

```
NSUncaughtExceptionHandler*
  NSGetUncaughtExceptionHandler( )
void NSSetUncaughtExceptionHandler
  (NSUncaughtExceptionHandler*)
```
> > Use these methods to retrieve or set the function the runtime calls for unhandled exceptions. The default function provided by the runtime writes an error message to stderr and exits the program.

A Cocoa exception handling example

The following example illustrates raising and handling an exception within the Cocoa framework. The example explicitly raises an exception in order to demonstrate how that's

---

done, but be aware that the Objective-C runtime can also implicitly raise exceptions.

```
1  NS_DURING
2    NSException* ex =
3      [[NSException alloc]
4        initWithName:@"ExceptionName"
5            reason:@"description"
6          userInfo:nil];
7    [ex raise];
8  NS_HANDLER
9    if ([[localException name]
10       isEqualToString:@"ExceptionName"])
11     // Handle exception.
12   else
13     [localException raise];
14 NS_ENDHANDLER
```

Line 1. Start the try block with the **NS_DURING** macro.

Line 2. Create an exception instance.

Line 4. Exceptions are distinguished—in code—by their names. Cocoa defines 22 names stored in global variables such as NSRangeException. You can use one of these or provide your own name.

Line 5. The reason can be any string. In contrast with the name, it's meant to be read by people, so make it descriptive.

Line 6. The user info is an instance of NSDictionary—a class that provides a mapping between key-value pairs. You can use this to provide detailed information about the error.

Line 7. You raise an exception by calling its raise method.

Line 8. The **NS_HANDLER** macro ends the try block and starts the handler.

Line 9. Inside the handler, the variable localException is defined. Use its name to decide what to do about it.

Line 11. This part is up to you.

Line 13. If you can't recover from the error, continue the exception by raising it again. This is optional.

Line 14. The **NS_ENDHANDLER** macro ends the handler section, and the exception-aware section as a whole.

Runtime Environment

When your Objective-C program is running, certain structures and services are always set up for you, even though you don't specifically ask for them. These serve as the counterpart to the compiler: together the compiler and the runtime implement the features that Objective-C adds to C. Most languages include runtime environments; Objective-C is distinctive in exposing a good part of its runtime in a public programming interface.

The runtime's interfaces are in header files that will be present in any installation of *gcc*. (For example, in Darwin they reside at */usr/include/objc*. Check your compiler's default include paths to locate these files.) You can also download the source code for the runtime; examining it is a good way to learn more about how dynamic languages are implemented.

Class Objects

Class objects are objects that represent at runtime the classes a program is using. Because they function in the same way as regular objects—you can send them messages and use them in expressions—Objective-C unifies the treatment of classes and their instances.

Class objects are also called factory objects, because in their most common usage you send them the +alloc message to create other objects.

Class objects are set up by the Objective-C compiler and initialized at runtime before your code needs to use them. To get a class object from an instance, use the -class method. For example, given an instance created this way:

```
Circle* c = [Circle new];
```

you can retrieve the class object of that instance like this:

```
Class circleClass = [c class];
```

Sending a message to a class object is common enough that it has a shortcut: just name the class as the receiver, as you do when you invoke +alloc.

In the Objective-C runtime all regular objects start with an isa field, pointing to their class object. The class object contains (or refers to) the instance methods that the object can respond to. In addition each class object has a super_class pointer which refers to the parent class object. For root classes—those that have no parents—super_class is set to **Nil**. Figure 1 illustrates how isa and super_class work together to define the inheritance-chain for an object of class C, which inherits from class B and the root class.

Runtime method dispatch for regular objects follows this sequence:

1. Follow the receiver's isa member to its class object.
2. Search for the method in the class object's method list.
3. If the method is not found, follow the class object's super_class pointer to the parent class.
4. Repeat steps 2–3 until the method is found, or the root class's super_class pointer (which is **Nil**) is evaluated.
5. If the message is still not handled, call the object's -forward:: method. Both Object and NSObject provides this method. (NSObject's version is private.) The default forwarding behavior is to abort the program.
6. If the object has no forwarding method, the program exits with an error.

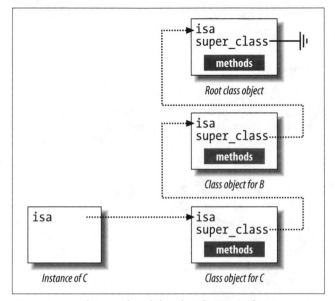

Figure 1. isa and super_class define the inheritance chain

The call to the forwarding method completes the method dispatcher's role in performing the original method call: it has now been transformed into a different call (which is dispatched with the same mechanism). The "Forwarding Messages" section describes the subsequent steps in processing an unhandled message.

Metaclass Objects

If instance methods are stored in class objects, then where are class methods stored? Class objects themselves have other objects to store the methods they respond to; these are called *metaclass objects*.

Like regular objects, class objects point to their metaclass objects with an isa field.

This design allows class method invocation and lookup to proceed exactly the same way as for instance methods. Class objects stand on an equal footing with other objects in Objective-C: you can assign them to variables declared as **id**, send messages to them, and they inherit (class) methods from their ancestors.

The runtime relation between classes and their metaclasses is illustrated in Figure 2.

Metaclass objects are identical in structure to class objects. However, their isa pointers all refer to the root metaclass. This is a practical measure to forestall the need for an infinite hierarchy of meta-metaclasses. (Effectively, the root class is the meta-metaclass of all its descendants.) Since you don't normally use metaclass objects, this is not a major blemish on the consistency of Objective-C.

Figure 2 shows one other distinctive asymmetry in the otherwise uniform structure of the runtime environment: the root metaclass's super_class pointer refers to the root class

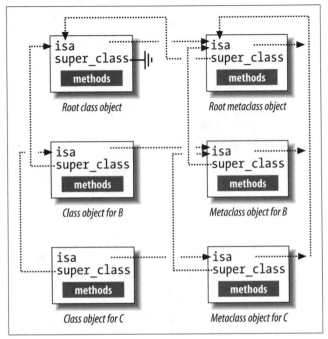

Figure 2. Classes and their metaclasses

object. This means that class objects behave as if they are instances of their root class: class objects will respond not only to their own class messages and those of their parent classes (including those of the root), but also to instance messages of the root class.

Selectors

For efficiency, method dispatch doesn't look up method names with string comparisons. Instead method names are mapped one-to-one with selectors—variables of type **SEL**. This mapping is known to both the compiler and the runtime system. If you want pass a method around as a parameter and invoke it through that parameter, you can use a **SEL** along with one of the -perform: methods. (The "Methods" section gives an example of this.)

Protocol Objects

The runtime also defines objects for each protocol in your program. You can retrieve these objects using the **@protocol** directive:

```
Protocol* p = @protocol(ProtocolName);
```

You can't do much with a protocol instance except pass it to root class methods that take protocols as parameters, or send the -conformsTo: message to it in order to see whether it conforms to yet another protocol.

Root Classes

A root class is one with no parent class. Objective-C allows multiple root classes, but you are most likely to use one supplied with your compiler.

All Objective-C distributions provide a root class called Object. This section describes the Object supplied with the GNU runtime. The Object class provided by Darwin is similar, but Darwin users will be more likely to use the NSObject root class that comes with the Cocoa class library. (The GNUstep library also provides an NSObject root class almost identical to Cocoa's.) This section describes the fields and methods of both Object and NSObject.

Both classes provide access to Objective-C features like reflection, memory management, and archiving. Most of the classes you write will inherit from one of these classes, so your objects will be able to use these features.

Fields

Both Object and NSObject declare only one field, isa, whose type is Class. This field is inherited by all their descendants, which is critical to the operation of inheritance and message dispatch. It points to the class object representing the instance's class. See the "Runtime Environment" section earlier in this book.

Methods

Root class methods are accessible from any object that derives from the class—usually all regular objects in a program. In addition, root class instance methods can be called on class objects for it and its subclasses—in other words, class objects appear to be instances of their root class. (The runtime arranges for this; see "Metaclass Objects" under "Runtime Environment.")

Because you can call root class instance methods on class objects, the behavior of some instance methods described here has several distinct, though consistent, cases:

- The receiver is a regular object.
- The receiver is a class object.
- The receiver is a metaclass object (in the GNU runtime, where metaclass objects are distinguished from class objects).

The root class method descriptions point these issues out where useful.

Some root class methods are meant to be overridden; others should not be. The following sections note where you may or must override a method.

NOTE

Many root class methods (e.g., -respondsTo:) return information about the receiver even when it's an instance of a subclass. This makes it look like they are automatically rewritten in each subclass, or that your classes should override them. In fact, the root class's implementation makes use of runtime reflection to provide the information required.

The Object Class

This section describes the methods provided by the GNU Object class. The source code for these methods, available in *Object.m*, gives a valuable view of how the Objective-C runtime works.

Creating, copying, and freeing objects

Object provides the following methods to manage the memory used for objects. You should never use the C functions malloc( ) and free( ) to manage Objective-C objects. The earlier "Object Lifecycle" section discusses how to use these methods.

+(**id**)new
   Calls +alloc on the class, then -init on the resulting instance, and returns the result.

+(**id**)alloc
   Allocates, clears, and returns a pointer to memory for a new instance of the receiver. Returns **nil** on failure.

+(**id**)initialize

> Returns **self**. The runtime calls this method before any
> instances of the receiving class are created. Override to
> perform class-specific setup.

-(**id**)init

> Returns **self**. This is the designated initializer for Object.

-(**id**)copy

> Calls -shallowCopy then -deepen on the resulting
> instance, and returns the result. In Object this is the same
> as -shallowCopy.

-(**id**)shallowCopy

> Returns a copy of the receiver. Fields that are pointers are
> not traversed, just duplicated in the new copy.

-(**id**)deepen

> Returns **self**. Override to replace all fields that are point-
> ers with new values. Otherwise, -deepCopy and -copy
> won't function correctly.

-(**id**)deepCopy

> Calls -copy and returns the result.

-(**id**)free

> Releases the memory occupied by the receiver. Also
> zeroes the isa pointer of the object. If the object is sent a
> message at this stage, an immediate runtime error will
> occur. (Once the memory has been reused, anything can
> happen.) Override to release other resources held by the
> receiver.

Identifying objects and classes

Use the following methods to find out about an object's
identity, and to compare it with other objects:

-(Class)class

- If the receiver is a regular object, returns the class
  object for the receiver's class.
- If the receiver is a class object, returns the receiver.

-(Class)superClass

- If the receiver is a regular object, returns the class object for the parent class of the receiver's class, or **nil** if the receiver's class is a root class.

- If the receiver is a class object, returns the class object for the receiver's parent class, or **nil** if the receiver represents a root class.

-(MetaClass)metaClass

- If the receiver is a regular object, returns the meta-class object for the metaclass of the receiver's class.

- If the receiver is a class object, returns the metaclass object for the metaclass of the receiver.

-(**const char***)name

Returns the name of the receiver's class.

-(**id**)self

Returns the receiver. You can get a class object from the class's name with this method:

```
Class classobj = [MyClass self];
```

-(**unsigned int**)hash

Returns an integer that can be used to store the object in a hash table. If two objects are equal (as reported by -isEqual:) they will have the same hash value. However, two unequal objects may also share the same hash value.

-(**BOOL**)isEqual:(**id**)obj

Returns **YES** if the receiver and obj are equal as pointers, otherwise returns **NO**. Override to implement another relation, such as equality of contents.

-(**int**)compare:(**id**)obj

Returns one of the following values:

- 0, if [**self** isEqual:obj] returns **YES**.
- -1, if the receiver's value (as a pointer) is less than that of obj.

- 1, if the receiver's value (as a pointer) is greater than that of *obj*.

Override this method if you want to compare your objects in a different way.

Testing object type

Objective-C minimizes the differences between regular and class objects, but sometimes it is helpful to know which is which. In addition, the GNU runtime distinguishes between class and metaclass objects. The following methods let you find out from an object what kind it is:

-(**BOOL**)isInstance
> Returns **YES** if the receiver is a regular object, otherwise **NO**.

-(**BOOL**)isClass
> Returns **YES** if the receiver is a class object, otherwise **NO**.

-(**BOOL**)isMetaClass
> Returns **YES** if the receiver is a metaclass object, otherwise **NO**.

Testing inheritance and conformance

Use the following methods to find out an object's place in the inheritance hierarchy:

-(**BOOL**)isKindOf:(Class)*classObj*
- If the receiver is an ordinary object, returns **YES** if the receiver's class is *classObj* or a descendant of it, **NO** otherwise.
- If the receiver is a class object, returns **YES** if *classObj* is the immediate metaclass of the receiver, **NO** otherwise.
- If the receiver is a metaclass, returns **NO**.

-(**BOOL**)isKindOfClassNamed: (**const char***)*className*
> Same as -isKindOf:, but takes as a parameter the name of a class instead of a class object.

-(**BOOL**)isMemberOf:(Class)*classObj*

- If the receiver is an ordinary object, returns **YES** if the receiver's class is *classObj*, otherwise **NO**.
- If the receiver is a class or metaclass object, returns **NO**.

-(**BOOL**)isMemberOfClassNamed:(**const char***)*className*
Same as -isMemberOf:, but takes as a parameter the name of a class instead of a class object.

-(**BOOL**)conformsTo:(Protocol*)*prot*
Returns **YES** if the class of the receiver adopts the protocol directly, or if that class directly or indirectly inherits from another class that does.

Information about methods

Use the instance methods listed here to ask regular objects about instance methods, and class objects about class methods.

+(**BOOL**)instancesRespondTo:(**SEL**)*sel*;
Returns **YES** if instances of the receiving class respond to the selector *sel*, otherwise **NO**. Does not take forwarding into account.

-(**BOOL**)respondsTo:(**SEL**)*sel*
Returns **YES** if the receiver responds to the selector *sel*, otherwise **NO**. Does not take forwarding into account.

+(**struct** objc_method_description*)
descriptionForInstanceMethod:(**SEL**)*sel*
If instances of the receiving class handle the method specified by *sel*, this method returns a pointer to a description of the method; otherwise it returns a **NULL** pointer.

The return type is defined as follows in *objc-api.h*:

```
struct objc_method_description {
  SEL name;
  char* types;
};
```

The first member of the structure will be of little use since you already have the selector. The second points to a zero-terminated character string. The string takes the form of type specifiers (as returned by the **@encode** directive) for the return and parameter types, interleaved with numbers describing offsets of the parameters in the stack frame.

-(**struct** objc_method_description*)
descriptionForMethod:(**SEL**)*sel*

> If the receiver handles the method specified by *sel*, this method returns a pointer to a description of the method; otherwise it returns a **NULL** pointer.

+(**IMP**)instanceMethodFor:(**SEL**)*sel*

> If instances of the receiving class handle the method specified by *sel*, this method returns a pointer to the implementation of the specified method; otherwise a **NULL** pointer. You can use this to get a pointer to a method you want to call directly. See "Optimizing Method Calls" for an example.

-(**IMP**)methodFor:(**SEL**)*sel*

> If the receiver handles the method specified by *sel*, this method returns a pointer to the method's code; otherwise a **NULL** pointer.

Sending messages

Use the following methods to send messages when you won't know until runtime which message to send:

-(**id**)perform:(**SEL**)*sel*

> Sends to the receiver the message specified by the selector *sel*. Since selectors can be assigned to variables, one part of your code can tell another which message to send.

-(**id**)perform:(**SEL**)*sel*
>   with:(id)*obj1*

> The same as -perform: but also provides the argument *obj1* to the method being called.

```
-(id)perform:(SEL)sel
      with:(id)obj1
      with:(id)obj2
```
The same as -perform: but also provides two arguments to the method being called.

```
-(retval_t)performv:(SEL)sel
                   :(arglist_t)args
```
Like the -perform: methods, but takes a variable-length parameter list. Call this method inside your class's -forward:: method to delegate the message to another object.

The return type is a typedef for **void***. The second parameter describes the parameter types and values. You can treat this as an opaque type; its declaration is in *encoding.h*.

```
-(retval_t)forward:(SEL)sel
                  :(arglist_t)args
```
Invokes -doesNotRecognize. Override as described in "Forwarding Messages" to implement message forwarding. The parameter types are the same as for -performv::.

Posing

The following methods let you change the inheritance hierarchy at runtime:

```
+(id)poseAs:classObj
```
Substitutes the receiver for the class represented by *classObj*. The receiver must be a subclass of the class represented by *classObj*. The receiver can't declare any new fields. Call this method before creating any instances of the class represented by *classObj* or sending it any messages.

This is a way, similar to using categories, to add or override methods to an existing class. In contrast with a category, the posing class can send a message to **super**, which will execute the method in the class represented by *classObj*.

```
-(Class)transmuteClassTo:(Class)classObj
```
Sets the isa pointer of the receiver to *classObj*, and returns the previous value of the pointer. This effectively converts the receiver to an instance of the class represented by *classObj*. This will only work if the receiver's class is a descendant of the class represented by *classObj*, and instances of the two classes have the same size. If the call fails, it returns **nil**.

Enforcing intentions

Each method in the following list generates a runtime error. In each case, when you call the method, pass in the _cmd variable, which the runtime sets up to be the selector of the method you are in.

```
-(id)subclassResponsibility:(SEL)sel
```
Call this in a method that you require subclasses to override and implement.

```
-(id)notImplemented:(SEL)sel
```
Call this in a method that you have deliberately left unfinished.

```
-(id)shouldNotImplement:(SEL)sel
```
Call this in a method that you inherit (and override) but that makes no sense for your subclass to support.

Error handling

The following functions are used for error handling. See the "Runtime Errors" section for more information about their usage.

```
-(id)doesNotRecognize:(SEL)sel
```
Generates a runtime error by invoking the -error: method on **self**. The runtime sends this message to an object when the object has failed to respond to, or forward, a message.

`-(`**id**`)error:(`**const char**`*)`*format*`,...`

> Writes an error message to the system log (via the
> syslog( ) call) and exits the program. The runtime calls
> this method on **self** for a variety of error conditions.
> Override as described in "Runtime Errors" to customize
> error handling for a class.

Archiving

The GNU runtime provides the type TypedStream for reading
and writing objects to and from archives. The "Archiving
Objects" section describes this type and its use in saving and
restoring objects. The following methods support archiving:

`-(`**id**`)awake`

> Does nothing and returns **self**. Called by the runtime
> when an object has been reconstructed. Override to cus-
> tomize behavior when your objects are restored.

`-(`**id**`)write:(TypedStream*)`*stream*

> Writes the receiver to the specified stream.

`-(`**id**`)read:(TypedStream*)`*stream*

> Sets the receiver's fields by reading from the specified
> stream.

`+(`**id**`)setVersion:(`**int**`)`*version*

> Sets the class version number.

`+(`**int**`)version`

> Returns the class's version number, or zero if it has never
> been set.

`+(`**int**`)streamVersion:(TypedStream*)`*stream*

> Returns the version number of the typed stream.

The NSObject Class

NSObject supports most of the features of Object and adds
others. Often the NSObject version of a method will have a
more specifically typed return value. For example, -class is
declared to return a Class and not just an **id**.

In defining NSObject, Cocoa first declares the NSObject protocol. (It can be confusing that the class and protocol have the same name; they live in different namespaces.) This allows for other root classes. As long as they implement the NSObject protocol, they can be used in contexts that depend on the methods that NSObject implements.

The NSObject class implements the NSObject protocol along with other useful methods that its descendants may want but that are not part of the protocol and are not important for interchangeability.

NOTE

Cocoa also declares categories for NSObject, such as NSComparisonMethods, NSURLClient, and others, comprising dozens of additional methods. This handbook discusses a few of these categories (NSCoding, NSKeyValueCoding) separately, but omits them from this section.

In the following sections, the methods are grouped by topic, and marked as being part of the NSObject protocol or class.

Creating, copying, and freeing objects

The "Object Lifecycle" section discusses how to use the following methods, which create objects, copy objects, and free the memory used by objects:

+(**id**)alloc

Allocates, clears, and returns a pointer to memory for a new instance of the receiver. Memory comes from the default zone. Returns **nil** on failure. (NSObject class)

+(**id**)allocWithZone:(NSZone*)*zone*

Same as alloc, but uses a specific region of memory. NSZone is not a class but a C type that you should treat as opaque. You can get the zone of an object with the -zone method. You may improve cache performance by creating related objects in the same zone. Passing in a **nil** parameter means memory will be allocated from the default zone. (NSObject class)

+(**void**)initialize

Sent by the runtime before the class or any of its descendants is sent a message by the program. Each class gets the message exactly once, and superclasses get the message before subclasses. The NSObject implementation does nothing. Override (first passing the call to **super**) to perform per-class setup. (NSObject class)

-(**id**)init

Returns **self**. This is the designated initializer for NSObject. The "Object Lifecycle" section discusses overriding this method. (NSObject class)

+(**id**)new

Calls +alloc, then -init on the resulting instance, and returns the result. (NSObject class)

+(**id**)copyWithZone:(NSZone*)*zone*

Returns the receiver since class objects are unique. Ignores the parameter. Don't override. (NSObject class)

+(**id**)mutableCopyWithZone:(NSZone*)*zone*

Returns the receiver since class objects are unique. Ignores the parameter. Don't override. (NSObject class)

-(**id**)copy

Calls -copyWithZone: with a **nil** zone parameter. NSObject doesn't implement that method (only the class method of the same name) but many Cocoa classes do. Your class will have to implement -copyWithZone: in order to use -copy. The "Object Lifecycle" section discusses how to do this.

-(**id**)mutableCopy

Calls -mutableCopyWithZone: with a **nil** zone parameter. NSObject doesn't implement that method (only the class method of the same name) but many Cocoa classes do. Your class will have to implement -mutableCopyWithZone in order to use -mutableCopy. The "Object Lifecycle" section discusses how to do this. (NSObject class)

-(**void**)dealloc
  Deallocates the memory used to store the receiver. Override to release any additional resources managed by your object. Don't call -dealloc directly if you are using retain/release memory management. (See the "Memory Management" section.) (NSObject class)

+(**void**)load
  Called by the runtime when a class or category is set up for use by the runtime. Deprecated in favor of the +initialize method. (NSObject class)

Identifying objects and classes

Use the following methods to find out about an object's identity, and to compare it with other objects:

-(Class)class
  Returns the class object for the receiver's class. (NSObject protocol)

-(Class)superclass
  Returns the class object of the receiver's parent class. (NSObject protocol)

-(NSString*)description
  Returns a string describing the state of the receiver. The NSObject implementation prints the class name and the runtime address of the instance. Override to provide a string the runtime will use when you print an object using the %@ formatting descriptor with NSLog(). (NSObject protocol)

-(**id**)self
  Returns the receiver. You can get a class object from the class's name with this method:

      Class circleClass = [Circle self];

  (NSObject protocol)

-(**unsigned**)hash

> Returns an integer that can be used to store the object in a hash table. If two objects are equal (as reported by the -isEqual: method) they will have the same hash value. However, two unequal objects may also share the same hash value. (NSObject protocol)

-(**BOOL**)isEqual:(**id**)object

> Returns **YES** if the receiver and object are equal as pointers, otherwise returns **NO**. Override to provide different semantics, such as equality of contents. (NSObject protocol)

+(Class)class

> Returns the class object that represents the receiver, not (as you might expect) the metaclass object of the metaclass of the receiver. This means that [MyClass class] and [MyClass self] return the same value; the second expression is probably more clear. (NSObject class)

+(NSString*)description

> Returns the name of the class. (NSObject class)

+(**void**)setVersion:(**int**) version

> Sets the class version number. (NSObject class)

+(**int**)version

> Returns the class's version number, or zero if it has never been set. (NSObject class)

+(Class)superclass

> Returns the class object representing the receiver's parent class. (NSObject class)

Testing inheritance and conformance

Use the following methods to find out about an object's place in the inheritance hierarchy:

+(**BOOL**)conformsToProtocol:(Protocol*)*prot*

> Returns **YES** if the receiver adopts *prot* directly or inherits directly or indirectly from another class that does. (NSObject class)

-**(BOOL)**isKindOfClass:(Class)*C*

- If the receiver is an ordinary object, returns **YES** if the receiver's class is represented by *C* or is a descendant of the class represented by *C*, **NO** otherwise.

- If the receiver is a class object, returns **YES** if *C* represents NSObject, **NO** otherwise. (This is consistent with the special property that class objects appear to be instances of the root object class.)

- If the receiver is a metaclass object, returns **YES** if *C* represents NSObject or NSObject's metaclass, **NO** otherwise.

(NSObject protocol)

-**(BOOL)**isMemberOfClass:(Class) *C*

Is part of the NSObject protocol, and does one of the following:

- If the receiver is an ordinary object, returns **YES** if *C* represents the receiver's class, otherwise **NO**.

- If the receiver is a class object, returns **YES** if *C* represents the receiver's metaclass, otherwise **NO**.

- If the receiver is a metaclass object, returns **YES** if *C* represents NSObject's metaclass, otherwise **NO**.

(NSObject protocol)

-**(BOOL)**conformsToProtocol:(Protocol*)*prot*

Returns **YES** if the class of the receiver adopts the protocol directly, or directly or indirectly inherits from another class that does. (NSObject protocol)

-**(BOOL)**isProxy

Returns **NO**. (The NSProxy class also implements this method, and returns **YES**.) (NSObject protocol)

Information about methods

Use the instance methods listed here to ask regular objects about instance methods, and class objects about class methods.

+(**BOOL**)instancesRespondToSelector:(**SEL**)*sel*
> Returns **YES** if instances of the receiving class respond to the selector *sel*, otherwise **NO**. Does not take forwarding into account. (NSObject class)

+(**IMP**)instanceMethodForSelector:(**SEL**)*sel*
> If instances of the receiving class handle the method specified by *sel*, returns a pointer to the implementation of the specified method. You can use this to get a pointer to a method you want to call directly. The section "Optimizing Method Calls" gives an example.
>
> The Cocoa documentation says that if instances of the receiving class do not handle the specified method, a runtime error occurs. Instead, an apparently valid pointer is returned. You should use code like the following to test for errors:
>
> ```
> IMP imp = NULL;
> if ([ClassName instancesRespondToSelector:sel])
>   imp = [ClassName
>            instanceMethodForSelector:sel];
> ```
>
> After executing these instructions, *imp* will still be **NULL** if the class's instances do not handle the method specified by *sel*. (NSObject class)

+(NSMethodSignature*)
instanceMethodSignatureForSelector:(**SEL**)*sel*
> If instances of the receiving class handle the method specified by *sel*, returns a description of the method's signature for the specified method; otherwise returns **nil**. (NSObject class)

-(**IMP**)methodForSelector:(**SEL**)*sel*
> If the receiver handles the method specified by *sel*, this method returns a pointer to the method's code. You can use this to get a pointer to a method you want to call directly. The section "Optimizing Method Calls" gives an example.
>
> The Cocoa documentation says that if the receiver does not handle the specified method, a runtime error occurs.

Instead, an apparently-valid pointer is returned. You should use code like the following to test for errors:

```
IMP imp = NULL;
if ([obj respondsToSelector:sel])
    imp = [obj methodForSelector:sel];
```

After executing these instructions, *imp* will still be **NULL** if the receiver does not handle the method specified by *sel*. (NSObject class)

-(NSMethodSignature*)methodSignatureForSelector:(**SEL**)*sel*
> If the receiver handles the method specified by *sel*, this method returns a description of the method; otherwise it returns **nil**. (NSObject class)

-(**BOOL**)respondsToSelector:(**SEL**)*sel*
> Returns **YES** if the receiver responds to the selector sel; otherwise **NO**. Does not take forwarding into account. (NSObject protocol)

Sending messages

Use the following methods to send messages when you won't know until runtime which message to send:

-(**id**)performSelector:(**SEL**)*sel*
> Sends to the receiver the message specified by the selector *sel*. Since selectors can be assigned to variables, one part of your code can tell another which message to send.

-(**id**)performSelector:(**SEL**)*sel*
>   withObject:(**id**)*obj1*
> The same as -performSelector:, but also provides the argument *obj1* to the method being called.

-(**id**)performSelector:(**SEL**)*sel*
>   withObject:(**id**) *obj1*
>   withObject:(**id**)*obj2*
> The same as -performSelector:, but also provides two arguments to the method being called. If you need to pass more than two parameters, construct an

NSInvocation instance. The "Forwarding Messages" section gives an example. (NSObject protocol)

-(**void**)forwardInvocation:(NSInvocation*)*inv*
Invokes -doesNotRecognizeSelector:. The "Forwarding Messages" section describes how to override this to implement message forwarding. (NSObject class)

Posing

This method lets you modify the inheritance hierarchy at runtime:

+(**void**)poseAsClass:(Class)*classObj*
Substitutes the receiver for the class represented by *classObj*. The receiver must be a subclass of the class represented by *classObj*. The receiver can't declare any new fields. You should call this method before creating any instances of the class represented by *classObj* or sending it any messages.

This is a way, similar to using categories, to add or override methods to an existing class. In contrast with a category, the posing class can send a message to **super** and execute the method in the class represented by *classObj*. (NSObject class)

Error handling

The following functions are used for error handling. See the "Runtime Errors" section for more information about their usage.

-(**void**)doesNotRecognizeSelector:(**SEL**)*sel*
Raises an NSInvalidArgument exception. The runtime sends this message to an object when the object has failed to respond to or forward a message.

You can "un-implement" a method as follows:

```
-(void) methodName {
  [self doesNotRecognizeSelector: _cmd];
}
```

The class implementing this code will now behave as if it had no *methodName*.

You could also make an object handle any message without failing by overriding -doesNotRecognizeSelector:, but you should override -forwardInvocation: instead. (NSObject class)

Archiving

These are peripheral methods that support saving objects to disk and restoring them. The "Archiving Objects" section provides more information on this topic.

-(**id**)awakeAfterUsingCoder:(NSCoder*)*coder*
> Returns the receiver. Called by NSCoder when it has decoded the receiver. Override this to return some other object. You are responsible for releasing the receiver if you return a different object. (NSObject class)

-(Class)classForCoder
> Returns the receiver's class. Override to substitute another class during archiving. Called by NSCoder. (NSObject class)

-(**id**)replacementObjectForCoder:(NSCoder*)*coder*
> Returns **self**. Override to substitute another object for the receiver during archiving. Called by NSCoder. (NSObject class)

Reference counting

These methods support reference counting or return information about an object's allocation. See the "Memory Management" section for more information.

-(**id**)retain
> Increments the receiver's reference count and returns the receiver. (NSObject protocol)

-(**unsigned**)retainCount
> Returns the receiver's reference count. (NSObject protocol)

-(**oneway void**)release

    Decrements the receiver's reference count, and sends it the -dealloc message if the count reaches zero. The **oneway** keyword specifies that the caller can send the message asynchronously. (See the "Remote Messaging" section.) (NSObject protocol)

-(**id**)autorelease

    Adds the receiver to the current autorelease pool. Returns the receiver. (NSObject protocol)

-(NSZone*)zone

    Returns the memory zone in which the receiver was allocated. NSZone is not a class but a C type that you should treat as opaque. You can use the value returned by this method as a parameter to -copyWithZone: or -allocWithZone:. Cocoa creates a default zone when a program starts up, and normally you will allocate objects from this zone. You may be able to improve cache behavior by creating related objects in the same zone. See the Cocoa documentation for NSCreateZone( ) and related functions. (NSObject protocol)

Forwarding Messages

When an object is sent a message for which it has no method, the runtime system gives it another chance to handle the call before giving up. If the object supports a -forward:: method, the runtime calls this method, passing it information about the unhandled call. The return value from the forwarded call is propagated back to the original caller of the method.

Both Object and NSObject provide a -forward:: method, so all objects you are likely to encounter will behave as described in this section. In each case, the default behavior, implemented by the root class method, is to exit the program when an unhandled call is forwarded. Your classes can override this method to provide alternative behavior; common choices are to absorb the error or to redirect (forward) the unhandled message to another object, which is called a *delegate*.

Object Forwarding

The -forward:: method takes a selector and a second parameter that stores information about the parameters passed to the original (failed) method call.

The method supplied by GNU's Object sets off the following train of events:

1. -forward:: calls -doesNotRecognize: on **self**, passing the selector for the original method call.

2. -doesNotRecognize: in turn calls -error: passing a format string and the name of the original method call.

3. -error: logs an error message and aborts the program, unless you have overridden this method or installed an alternative error handler. The "Runtime Errors" section discusses this more.

If you want to just ignore messages that your class does not handle, you can override -forward:: to return **NULL**. To implement true forwarding for a class, override the -forward:: method in the following way:

```
1 -(retval_t)forward:(SEL)sel :(arglist_t)args {
2   if ([myDelegate respondsTo:sel])
3     return [myDelegate performv:sel :args]
4   else
5     return [super forward:sel :args];
6 }
```

Line 2. Check that the delegate actually handles the call. The -respondsTo: method does not itself take forwarding into account; if the delegate might itself have another delegate, you could skip this test and just execute line 3.

Line 3. Return the result of the forwarded call. Because you pass the parameters straight through, you don't need to know the details of the `arglist_t` type. Since `retval_t` is defined as a pointer type, you should not forward calls that return floating point numbers, structures, or other incompatible types.

Line 4. If you want to ignore any messages your delegate doesn't handle, you can skip this line and line 5.

Line 5. If your parent class may have an alternative way to forward the message, pass the message using the **super** keyword.

NSObject Forwarding

In Cocoa, the `-forward::` method is private to `NSObject`, so you shouldn't override it. The method sets off the following chain of events:

1. `-forward::` calls `-methodSignatureForSelector:` on **self**, passing the selector for the original method call. You will have to override this method to provide an `NSMethod-Signature` instance describing the signature of the method your forwarder will call.

NOTE

If you don't override `-methodSignatureForSelector:`, the inherited version will return **nil**. This will cause later stages of forwarding to raise an exception.

---

2. `-forward::` uses the signature returned from the previous call to construct an `NSInvocation` instance, and passes that to `-forwardInvocation:`.
3. The `-forwardInvocation:` method is the one you override to customize forwarding behavior. The version provided by `NSObject` simply calls `-doesNotRecognizeSelector:`.
4. The `NSObject` version of `-doesNotRecognizeSelector:` raises an `NSInvalidArgument` exception.

5. If your program doesn't handle the exception it will exit with return value 255. The "Runtime Errors" section describes how to handle exceptions.

To forward a message you must override two NSObject methods. If you want to just absorb the message, the process is simple, and different enough from the general case to merit a description here:

```
1 -(NSMethodSignature*)
2 methodSignatureForSelector:(SEL)sel {
3   return
4     [NSObject
5       instanceMethodSignatureForSelector:
6         @selector(self)];
7 }
8
9 -(void)forwardInvocation:(NSInvocation*)inv { }
```

Line 3. You must return a valid NSMethodSignature instance, even though the rest of your forwarding code will ignore it. You can be sure this example will succeed, because NSObject will always be present, with its -self method.

Line 9. Override this method to ignore its parameter and do nothing.

If you want to forward an unhandled method call to another object, you have to attend to more details. Again, you first override -methodSignatureForSelector: to return an object that encapsulates information about the method's interface:

```
1 -(NSMethodSignature*)
2 methodSignatureForSelector:(SEL)sel {
3   NSMethodSignature* sig =
4     [[self class]
5       instanceMethodSignatureForSelector:sel];
6   if (sig == nil)
7     sig = [myDelegate
8       methodSignatureForSelector:sel];
9   if (sig == nil)
10    sig = [Unused
11      instanceMethodSignatureForSelector:
12        @selector(unused)];
```

```
13    return sig;
14 }
```

Line 2. When this method is called for the purposes of forwarding, the parameter will be a selector for a method the receiver doesn't handle.

Line 3. Check to see if your object already handles the method. You do this because this method may be called for reasons other than preparing to forward a call your object doesn't handle. Since calling the method you are overriding will cause an infinite loop, you have to call the class instead.

Line 6. If your object does not handle the message, *sig* will be **nil** at this point and you can ask your delegate about the method's signature.

Line 9. If *sig* is still **nil** at this point, your delegate is not equipped to handle the forwarded message. (This would certainly be a programming error.) If you return **nil** your program will crash. Your best recovery strategy is to have a special-purpose class with a single method, unused anywhere in your program. Returning its method signature lets your -forwardInvocation: method detect that the delegate won't handle it, and instead ignore it.

Next you override -forwardInvocation: to redirect the call:

```
1 -(void)forwardInvocation:(NSInvocation*)inv {
2    if ([myDelegate respondsToSelector:
3                   [inv selector]])
4       [inv invokeWithTarget:myDelegate];
5    else
6       [super forwardInvocation:inv];
7 }
```

Line 1. The parameter contains information about the method call: the selector, parameter values and types, and return type.

Line 2. Check that the delegate actually handles the call.

Line 4. If the delegate will handle the call, forward the message.

Line 5. If you intend to just ignore messages that the delegate won't handle, you don't need this line or line 6.

Line 6. If your parent class may have an alternative way to forward the message, pass the invocation object to it using the **super** keyword.

Memory Management

The liveness of an object—whether or not it is referenced by other objects currently in use—is inherently a global property. This means that keeping track of object usage tempts you to breach the encapsulation and modularity of your program. There are several approaches you can use with Objective-C to help manage object lifecycles:

- Manual memory management, using the free functions provided by the Objective-C runtime
- Semi-automatic memory management, using root class reference-counting methods
- Automatic memory management, using third-party garbage collector tools

The programming tools and libraries you use may constrain you toward or away from some strategies. For example, the Cocoa class library uses reference counting; if your code uses Cocoa objects it will have to be written to manage those objects with reference counting, even if your own objects use a different mechanism.

Manual Memory Management

You can explicitly release the memory held by an object by calling its -free method (if it inherits from Object) or its -dealloc method (if it inherits from NSObject). It will be your responsibility to ensure that your program no longer needs the object.

In classes you write, the deallocation method should release any objects managed by the receiver, as well as any other kinds of resources (such as network sockets) the receiver holds. As with deciding to deallocate the receiver itself, it is your responsibility to ensure that your program no longer needs the objects the receiver will release. This is difficult enough that automatic management systems are becoming more prevalent.

Reference Counting

The Cocoa framework supports *reference counting*: a technique that associates with an object a count that describes how many references there are to the object in other code. When this count is positive, the object is in use; when the count reaches zero the object can be discarded and its memory reclaimed.

The count doesn't specify the users of the object. When an object has a reference count of one it means *some* other code uses it. If you release one object from memory but forget that it was maintaining a counted reference to another object, the runtime will never notice a discrepancy. For reference counting to be effective you must observe some conventions or design patterns when using its methods. This section gives guidelines for using the reference counting methods.

NOTE

The techniques described in this section apply to objects that are used in a single thread. If you share objects between multiple threads you will have to take more care in retaining and releasing objects, and possibly create per-thread autorelease pools. Multithreaded memory management is a complex topic outside the scope of this handbook.

Maintaining an object's reference count

Cocoa provides four root class methods, -retain, -release, -autorelease, and -retainCount, for using reference counting. (They are documented in the "Root Classes" section.) You don't have to override the methods, just inherit from NSObject and use them.

An object's reference count changes in the following ways:

- When an object is created, it starts out with a reference count of one.

- When an object receives a -retain message, its reference count is incremented by one. Call this method on an object to indicate that your code is using the object.

- When an object receives an -autorelease message, the runtime schedules a -release message to be sent when the current call stack exits. Call this method in the following situations:

  — To specify early in a method that an object may be released after the method exits, while ensuring that it will remain valid throughout the method's execution. This would be difficult to arrange manually if your method may raise an exception or has several exit points.

  — To return an object to a caller and ensure that it will not be released between the exit of a method and the resumption of the calling method (between which there may be many intervening scopes).

- When an object receives a -release message, its reference count is decremented by one. Call this method to indicate that your code is done using the object.

- The -release method also tests the reference count's value. If it is zero, the method sends the object a -dealloc message. You don't call -dealloc yourself.

These rules lead to the following rule of thumb:

The sum of the count of release and autorelease messages sent by your code to an object over its full lifetime should be one more than the number of retain messages.

(The releases outnumber the retains because an object's reference count starts at one, not zero.)

Using reference counting correctly calls for coordination when passing objects as parameters between scopes or threads. You need to know when the methods are called for you implicitly, and when to call them yourself. The following sections describe some of the most common situations and how to handle them.

Creating a new object

When you create the object yourself, by using an +alloc, -copy, or -mutableCopy method, you've already implicitly called -retain. The question then is when to release the object. Following are some common alternatives:

- You are immediately giving the object up (passing it back to a caller) and never getting it back again. Call -autorelease before returning it.
- You are storing it in a field or global. Call -release in the owning object's -dealloc method.

Receiving an object from another scope

You get an object as a parameter in a method, or from a class method whose name starts with the class name. In both cases, some other code is the owner, and may call -release based on criteria hidden from you. How you manage the object's reference depends on how you use it:

- You use the object only locally and do not expect it to become invalid. This will be the case with objects that aren't shared, for example new strings you get from NSString's method +stringWithString:. You don't need to retain or release it.

- You use the object locally, but some calls you make may indirectly cause it to be released. (For example, the owner of the object may replace it with a new object.) Call -retain and then -autorelease on the object before using it.
- You are storing it in a field or global. See the upcoming section "Replacing an already-stored object."

Returning an already-stored object

You are returning a value you didn't just create, for example, in a method that returns a field (a "getter"). In this case, you have the following choices for returning the object:

- If speed is critical and you know that there is only one autorelease pool in your thread, you can return the value directly.
- A more generally safe approach is to call -retain and then -autorelease on the field, and then return it. This prevents the object from being released as a side-effect of code that executes after the getter exits but before the caller has a chance to retain it.

Replacing an already-stored object

You are provided with a new object to replace an existing one, for example, in a method that sets a field (a "setter"). There are a few equally safe solutions:

- Call -autorelease on the existing object, then retain the provided one, and assign the retained or copied value to the field.
- Compare the provided object with the existing one. If they are equal (as pointers) do nothing. Otherwise release the existing object, retain the provided one, and assign it to the field.
- Call -retain on the provided object, -release on the existing one, then assign the retained or copied value to the field.

For example, to use the third approach for a setter for a field named *ownedObj*, your setter will look like:

```
-(void)setOwnedObj:(id)newObj {
    [newObj retain];
    [ownedObj release];
    ownedObj = newObj;
}
```

Don't call -copy instead of -retain in a setter. It is safe as far as memory usage goes, but prevents your caller from sharing the value; by contrast, when you use -retain a caller can copy the new object explicitly and pass the copy to the setter.

Deallocating an object

When a call to -release sets your object's reference count to zero, the -release method will also call the object's -dealloc method. In that method, you should release all other objects (e.g., fields) and resources that your object is retaining. If other code that shares those objects is retaining them (as it should), this will be safe.

You can make your -dealloc method safer in the face of outside code that may have bugs by calling -autorelease on your retained objects. This leaves the autoreleased objects still available until the current call stack finishes. However, it is probably a design mistake if code remaining in the call stack depends on these objects, and using -autorelease may just hide this rather than solve it.

Retain cycles

Reference counting can break down when there is a closed loop in the graph of object references. In this case a group of mutually referent objects may be garbage (i.e., unreachable from your program) but with positive reference counts. You don't have to avoid such structures, but make sure that you only apply the counting in one direction. When two objects refer to each other, decide which is the "owner" and let it retain the other object, but not vice versa.

Garbage Collection

Garbage collection is a memory management technique that fully automates the release and reuse of object memory. A garbage collector keeps track of which objects are reachable from running code; unreachable objects (those with no references, direct or indirect) are released.

The *gcc* compiler emits code that can be linked with the Boehm garbage collector (an open source garbage collector for C-based languages). This library augments the standard C function malloc() with code that sets up tracking information for object pointers, and replaces the function free() with an empty body. The garbage collector runs concurrently in your program, releasing objects only when they are no longer reachable by executing code. The Boehm garbage collector will even correctly deal with cycles of mutually-referring but unreachable objects.

To use the garbage collector, you download and compile it as a library for your platform, and link it with your Objective-C program. You can get the code, and instructions on how to install it, at *http://www.hpl.hp.com/personal/Hans_Boehm/gc/*.

NOTE

Garbage collection and reference counting can't run in the same program. The Cocoa library is built around the retain/release reference counting design, so you can't use a garbage collector in Cocoa-based programs.

Archiving Objects

Saving and restoring objects is made easier by Objective-C's facilities for *reflection*—inspecting at runtime the structure of instances and classes. Objects can be pre-designed at build-time, encoded, and saved as resources for reconstruction at runtime. The runtime state of objects can similarly be saved and restored in documents or other files. An object's values are stored along with type information necessary to restore a fully functioning instance.

Archiving Descendants of Object

To save and restore descendants of Object, you can use its methods -write: and -read:, along with some functions provided by the runtime and a helper class called TypedStream.

For example, suppose your class declares an interface like this:

```
@interface MyClass : Object {
  AnotherClass* obj;
  int i;
}
...
@end
```

To add the fields that MyClass declares to a stream that will be written to an archive, implement the following method:

```
1 -(id)write:(TypedStream*)stream {
2   [super write:stream];
3   objc_write_types(stream, "@i", obj, &i);
4   return self;
5 }
```

Line 1. Override the root class method -write:.

Line 2. Call the parent class method to write the fields declared in the parent.

Line 3. Call the runtime function objc_write_types(). The second parameter is a concatenation of descriptors for the types of fields you are writing. These are one-character strings, the same as those used by the **@encode** directive. They are listed in *objc-api.h*.

To read the fields of MyClass from a stream that has been read from an archive, implement the following method:

```
1 -(id)read:(TypedStream*)stream {
2   [super read:stream];
```

```
3    objc_read_types(stream, "@i", obj, &i);
4    return self;
5  }
```

Line 1. Override the root class method -read:.

Line 2. Call the parent class method to read the fields declared in the parent.

Line 3. Call the runtime function objc_read_types( ). The second parameter is a concatenation of descriptors for the types of the fields you are reading. These are one-character strings, the same as those used by the **@encode** directive, and declared in *objc-api.h*.

Line 4. Return the instance once it's been read.

To use these methods, you create an instance of TypedStream and pass it to your object's -read: and -write: methods. For example, this code will save an object to a file on disk:

```
1  MyClass* obj = [MyClass new];
2  TypedStream* stream =
3    objc_open_typed_stream_for_file("storage",
4      OBJC_WRITEONLY);
5  [obj write:stream];
6  objc_close_typed_stream(stream);
```

Line 1. Create the object in whatever way you choose.

Line 2. Create a TypedStream instance.

Line 3. Call the runtime function open_typed_stream_for_file( ). The first parameter is a filename.

Line 4. Here the second parameter to the objc_open_typed_stream_for_file method specifies that you will be writing to a file.

Line 5. Pass the stream to the object's -write: method. The object's declared and inherited fields are written to a file.

Line 6. Close the stream.

To retrieve the saved object, you can use the following code:

```
1 TypedStream* stream =
2   objc_open_typed_stream_for_file("storage",
3     OBJC_READONLY);
4 MyClass* obj = [[MyClass alloc] read:stream];
5 objc_close_typed_stream(stream);
```

Line 1. Create a TypedStream instance.

Line 2. Call the runtime function open_typed_stream_for_file( ). The first parameter is a filename.

Line 3. Here the second parameter to the objc_open_typed_stream_for_file method specifies that you will be reading from a file.

Line 4. Allocate space for your object, then set its fields by passing the stream to the object's -read: method.

Line 5. Close the stream.

The GNU runtime provides more functions for managing object storage and retrieval. See the documentation for your distribution for more information.

Archiving Descendants of NSObject

The Cocoa framework uses the term "coding" for the process of translating objects to a saveable form. Cocoa declares an NSCoding protocol, and provides an NSCoder class that saves and restores objects that implement the protocol. NSObject does not itself implement NSCoding; to use archiving, you must implement the NSCoding protocol in your classes.

The NSCoding protocol consists of two methods: initWithCoder: and encodeWithCoder:. These exhibit the same structure as initializers: you first send the same message to **super**, then proceed to encode or decode the fields of your object, following the same order in each method. Your objects don't have to pay any more attention than that to the details of constructing or interpreting an object's stored form.

For example, suppose your class declares an interface like this:

```
@interface MyClass : NSObject {
   AnotherClass* obj;
   int i;
}
...
@end
```

To save the fields of MyClass, implement the following method:

```
1 -(void)encodeWithCoder:(NSCoder*)coder {
2   // [super encodeWithCoder:coder];
3   [coder encodeObject:obj];
4   [coder encodeValueOfObjCType:@encode(int)
5                         at:&i];
6 }
```

Line 1. Declare the method as specified by the NSCoding protocol. Cocoa's archiving methods will pass in the coder object to your encode method.

Line 2. Call **super** only if the parent class also implements the NSCoding protocol. In this example, the parent class is NSObject, which doesn't implement the protocol, so this line of code is commented out.

Line 3. If the field is an Objective-C object, pass it to the coder using the -encodeObject: method.

Line 4. If the field is a C type, use the -encodeValueOfObjCType method shown here. The @encode

---

directive constructs a string describing the structure of the specified type, which tells the coder how to process the value. The coder stores the string along with the value to facilitate decoding.

Line 5. Instead of directly passing the value you want to store, you pass its address.

To read the fields of *MyClass*, implement the following method:

```
 1 -(void)initWithCoder:(NSCoder*)coder {
 2   if (self = [super initWithCoder:coder] {
 3     int version =
 4       [coder versionForClassName:@"MyClass"];
 5     // Check version here.
 6     obj = [[coder decodeObject] retain];
 7     [coder decodeValueOfObjCType:@encode(int)
 8                              at:&i];
 9   }
10 }
```

Line 1. Declare the method to conform to the NSCoding protocol. Cocoa's archiving methods will pass in the coder object to your decoding method.

Line 2. Call **super** only if the parent class also implements the NSCoding protocol. If the parent class does not implement the NSCoding protocol, call its designated initializer instead. In either case, assign the result to **self** because the parent class may return a different object than itself.

Lines 3, 4. Get the class's version number, which the coder automatically stores with the object information.

Line 5. Depending on the version number, you may have to vary the implementation of the rest of the method.

Line 6. To retrieve an Objective-C object, call the coder's -decodeObject method. You must decode objects in the same order you encoded them in the -encodeWithCoder: method.

When you get a value from -decodeObject, you should call -retain on it. The NSCoder will also be retaining the value until it is no longer needed by that class, at which time NSCoder will release it.

Line 7. To retrieve a field that is a C type, use the form shown here. The **@encode** directive constructs a string telling the coder about the structure of the value it will be decoding.

Line 8. You must pass the address of the value you are restoring.

To use the archiving framework, the data you save and restore needs to have a *root object*. This isn't the same as a root class, but means an object from which all other objects are reachable through pointers. If you implement the NSCoding protocol as described here, the coding process will traverse all the connections and encode or decode all the data.

You set the encoding or decoding process off by calling class methods of NSArchiver and NSUnarchiver. For example, to encode data starting with object *rootObj*:

```
NSData* encoded =
    [NSArchiver archivedDataWithRootObject:rootObj];
```

To decode data back into a root object:

```
rootObj =
    [NSUnarchiver unarchiveObjectWithData:encoded];
```

The archiver objects create the NSCoder object and pass it to the NSCoding protocol methods of your objects.

There are many ways you can use the archiving framework, but the most common is to save and restore data using an NSDocument subclass. This class provides several methods for saving and restoring data through a root object. Most commonly, you will override -dataRepresentationOfType: and -loadDataRepresentation:ofType: to call the archiver and unarchiver methods. See your Cocoa documentation for more information on saving and restoring documents.

Key-Value Coding

Objective-C lets you call methods specified by variables at runtime using the selector mechanism. Key-value coding is a library facility that puts field access on the same dynamic footing: you can access an object's fields by naming them. For example, you could use the following code to retrieve the parent field of a window object:

```
Window* parentWind = [wind valueForKey:@"parent"];
```

Because you can pass a string variable to -valueForKey: as well as a literal value, this is another way your program's behavior can vary based on values that aren't known until runtime.

NSObject implements -valueForKey: method as part of the NSKeyValueCoding category, which declares methods for reading from and writing to the fields of objects. These methods store and retrieve Objective-C objects, so their primary use is in accessing objects. However, even if your fields are integers or other numeric types, you can still use key-value coding to retrieve and set them. The methods will take NSNumber objects and automatically convert them to set numeric fields, and return NSNumber objects when you read numeric fields.

Access Permissions

The key-value methods can bypass the access modifiers of the static language: you can read and write to private fields as easily as to public ones. This might seem like a violation of the object's declared interface. However, you can prevent key-value methods from bypassing your access modifiers by overriding +accessInstanceVariablesDirectly to return **NO**.

In addition, the key-value methods first search for an appropriate accessor method in your class before attempting to read from or write to a field directly. For example, the methods that read a field named field will look for accessor methods with the following names (the order will vary as described in the next section):

- getField
- field
- _getField
- _field

The key-value methods will take care of uppercasing the first letter of the field name before prepending get or set.

NOTE

Although the key-value methods will search for methods or fields whose names start with an underscore, Apple has reserved these names for its internal use. Your classes should not have methods or fields that start with an underscore.

If your class provides accessor methods with the appropriate names, they will be called even if they are private methods not declared in your class's interface.

NSKeyValueCoding Methods

The NSKeyValueCoding protocol declares (and NSObject implements) six methods that let your objects use key-value coding:

-(**id**)valueForKey:(NSString*)*key*
    Given the name of a field, returns the value stored in that field. If *key* is "field", -valueForKey: tries the following ways to get the associated value:

    1. Calls -getField, if it exists.
    2. Calls -field, if it exists.
    3. Calls -_getField, if it exists.
    4. Calls -_field, if it exists.
    5. Reads field, if it exists and direct access is allowed.
    6. Reads _field, if it exists and direct access is allowed.

If all of these fail, -valueForKey: calls -handleQuery-
WithUnboundKey: on your object.

-(**void**)takeValue:(**id**)*value*
    forKey:(NSString*)*key*

Given the (pointer to the) object, this method stores the
pointer to the object in the field of the receiver named by
the key. If *key* is "field", -takeValue:forKey: tries the following ways to set the associated value:

1. Calls -setField:, if it exists.
2. Calls -_setField:, if it exists.
3. Sets field, if it exists and direct access is allowed.
4. Sets _field, if it exists and direct access is allowed.

If all of these fail, -takeValue:forKey: calls
-handleTakeValue:forUnboundKey: on your instance.

- (**id**)storedValueForKey:(NSString*)*key*

Works like -valueForKey:, but with a possibly different
search sequence:

- If +useStoredAccessor returns **NO**, the sequence is the
  same as with -valueForKey:.
- If +useStoredAccessor returns **YES** (the default behavior), this method starts searching in reserved accessors (ones starting with underscores) first.

For example, if *key* is "field", and +useStoredAccessor
returns **YES**, -storedValueForKey: tries the following ways
to get the associated value:

1. Calls -_getField, if it exists.
2. Calls -_field, if it exists.
3. Reads _field, if it exists and direct access is allowed.
4. Reads field, if it exists and direct access is allowed.
5. Calls -getField, if it exists.
6. Calls -field, if it exists.

If all of these fail, -storedValueForKey: calls -handle-
QueryWithUnboundKey: on your instance.

The alternative search sequence supported by -storedValueForKey: facilitates using key-value coding for storing and retrieving objects from a database, when you want to bypass public accessors that may have side-effects.

```
-(void)takeStoredValue:(id)value
              forKey:(NSString*)key
```
Works like -takeValue:forKey:, but with a possibly different search sequence:

- If -useStoredAccessor return **NO**, the sequence is the same.
- If +useStoredAccessor returns **YES** (the default behavior), this method starts searching in reserved accessors (ones starting with underscore) first.

For example, if the key is field, and +useStoredAccessor returns **YES**, -takeStoredValue:forKey: tries the following ways to get the associated value:

1. Calls -_setField:, if it exists.
2. Sets _field, if it exists and direct access is allowed.
3. Sets field, if it exists and direct access is allowed.
4. Calls -setField:, if it exists.

If all of these fail, -takeStoredValue:forKey: calls -handleTakeValue:forUnboundKey: on your object.

```
+(BOOL)accessInstanceVariablesDirectly
```
The NSObject version returns **YES**. Override this in your class to affect the search sequence for the basic methods -valueForKey: and -takeValueForKey:.

```
+(BOOL)useStoredAccessor
```
The NSObject version returns **YES**. Override this in your class to affect the search sequence for the stored methods -storedValueForKey: and -takeStoredValue:forKey:.

Handling Key Lookup Failures

The category NSKeyValueCodingExceptions provides three methods for handling failures in the lookup sequence and other problems:

-(**id**)handleQueryWithUnboundKey:(NSString*)*key*
> Called when lookup fails for a getter (-valueForKey: or -storedValueForKey:) with the provided key. The default version of this method, provided in NSObject, raises an UnknownKeyException. Override this to handle things your way.

-(**void**)handleTakeValue:(**id**)*value*
> forUnboundKey:(NSString*)*key*
> Called when lookup fails for a setter (-takeValueForKey: or -takeStoredValueForKey:) with the provided key. The default version of this method, provided in NSObject, raises an UnknownKeyException. Override this to handle things your way.

-(**void**)unableToSetNilForKey:(NSString*)*key*
> Called when you pass **nil** in to a setter for a numeric field. NSObject's version raises an exception. Override this in your class if there is a plausible numeric value (zero, or an out-of-band value) to use.

Optimizing Method Calls

Objective-C's message-passing implementation of method calls is simple and flexible. What it sacrifices is the speed of a C++-style method call, or of a direct function call.

If you are writing time-critical code, you may want to relinquish the dynamic nature of the Objective-C method call for some extra speed. For example, if your code calls the same method on an object many times in a loop, you may not want to send a dynamic message each time you invoke the method. Objective-C provides a way for you to get a pointer

to the function implementing the method, and then call the
method via the pointer, bypassing the Objective-C method
dispatch process.

NOTE

If you only call a method once, you should use a standard Objective-C method call. This optimization's gain in
efficiency is directly related to the number of times you
invoke the method.

For example, suppose you want to send the following message to invoke a method that takes an integer and has no
return value:

```
[obj methodName:anInt];
```

You can replace this ordinary Objective-C method call with
the following code:

```
1 SEL sel = @selector(methodName:);
2 typedef void (*MpType) (id, SEL, int);
3 MpType mptr = (MpType) [obj methodFor:sel];
4 ...
5 mptr(obj, sel, anInt);
```

Line 1. Get the selector for the method you want to call. You
will use this both to acquire the method pointer and to use it.

Line 2. Define the type of your method pointer. This makes
line 3 easier to read. Recall that methods are just C functions
with two hidden parameters: the receiver and the selector.
Here, the type of mptr takes these into account, as well as the
return (**void**) and parameter (**int**) types of the method.

Line 3. Get the function pointer. If you already have the
receiver at hand (as in this example) you can use -methodFor:
(for descendants of Object) or -methodForSelector: (for
descendants of NSObject). If you don't have the receiver or an
object of the same type, you can call the class methods
+instanceMethodFor: (for subclasses of Object) or

`+instanceMethodForSelector:` (for subclasses of `NSObject`) on the class of the object whose method you will call.

Since these methods are declared to return an **IMP**, which is a pointer to a function whose signature is (**id**, **SEL**, ...) you need to cast to your own type the value it returns, to prevent compiler warnings at line 5.

Line 5. Use the function pointer as in C. Pass in the receiver and selector as the first two arguments. After you execute lines 1–3, line 5 will have the same effect as calling [*obj methodName:anInt*], but will execute faster. Typically this line will be in a loop.

Optimizing a method call in this manner only makes sense when you are going to invoke the method repeatedly, such as within a loop. Lines 1 through 3 represent a one-time setup that should be done prior to entering the loop. Line 5 is the optimized method call that would be used inside the loop.

Objective-C++

gcc is at once a compiler for C, Objective-C, and C++. You can intermix C++ and Objective-C code to some degree. To instruct the compiler that a file contains C++ code as well as Objective-C, use the file extension *.mm* or *.M* instead of *.m*.

Following are some ways in which C++ and Objective-C code can be used together:

- Objective-C objects can have fields that point to C++ objects, and vice versa.
- Objective-C code can call methods on C++ objects, and vice versa.
- Objective-C objects can have C++ objects (as opposed to pointers) as fields, but only if the C++ class has no virtual methods.

However, Objective-C and C++ are not completely compatible. Here are some things you can't do:

- Objective-C classes can't inherit from C++ classes, and vice versa.
- You can't declare Objective-C classes in C++ namespaces or templates, or vice versa.
- You can't use C++ keywords for Objective-C variable names.
- You can't call Objective-C methods with C++ syntax, or vice versa.

Finally, there are some restrictions that are imposed to avoid ambiguity:

- You can't use the name id as a C++ template name. If you could, the declaration id<TypeName> var could be either a C++ template declaration or an Objective-C declaration using a protocol.
- If you are passing a globally-scoped C++ variable to an Objective-C method, you need a space between the first and second colons. For example:

      [obj methodName: ::aGlobal].

Objective-C Resources

If you want to learn more about Objective-C, your options are more numerous than ever. Following are some text and Internet resources that expand on the topics outlined in this handbook.

http://www.ora.com/catalog/objectcpr
   Updates and corrections to this handbook.

http://www.faqs.org/faqs/computer-lang/Objective-C/faq/
   Frequently asked questions about Objective-C, and their answers.

http://developer.apple.com/techpubs/macosx/Cocoa/ObjectiveC/ObjC.pdf
> A document summarizing the Objective-C language, and providing examples of its use with the Cocoa libraries.

news://comp.lang.objective-c
> Usenet newsgroup for discussing Objective-C.

http://www.cetus-links.org/oo_objective_c.html
> Many helpful links to FAQs, tutorials, and other information about Objective-C.

http://gcc.gnu.org
> Web site for releases and documentation for GNU's *gcc* compiler.

http://developer.apple.com/techpubs/macosx/Cocoa/CocoaTopics.html
> Web site for documentation of the Cocoa class library.

http://www.gnustep.org
> Web site for releases and documentation for the GNUstep library, an open source version of Cocoa.

http://cocoa.mamasam.com
> A searchable archive that combines several Cocoa developer mailing lists.

Cocoa Programming for Mac OS X
> An introduction to both Objective-C and the Cocoa framework. By Aaron Hillegass. Addison-Wesley.

Learning Cocoa with Objective-C
> An introduction to both Objective-C and the Cocoa framework. By James Duncan Davidson. O'Reilly & Associates.

Cocoa Programming
> A more advanced guide to the Cocoa framework. By Scott Anguish, Erik Buck, and Donald A. Yacktman. SAMS.

Index

Symbols

-> (dereference operator), 19
... (ellipses), indicating variable-size
    parameter lists, 19
- (hyphen), marking instance
    methods with, 11, 16
+ (plus), marking class methods
    with, 11, 17

A

access modifiers, 10, 15
    bypassing, using key-value
      methods, 107
+accessInstanceVariablesDirectly
    method, 107, 110
accessors, 22
+alloc method, 48, 71, 80
    class objects and, 64
    retaining/releasing objects, 97
allocating memory, 47–49
+allocWithZone: method, 56, 80
ancestor initialization, 50
archiving objects, 100–106
    methods for, 79, 88
-autorelease method, 89, 96–99
-awake method, 79
-awakeAfterUsingCoder:
    method, 88

B

Boehm garbage collector, 100
BOOL type, 35
built-in types, 34
bycopy type qualifier, 34, 46
byref type qualifier, 34, 46

C

C++ and Objective-C,
    intermixing, 113
calling methods (see method calls)
categories, 26–29
    declaring, 21, 27
    implementing, 28
@class directive, 38
class libraries
    Cocoa (see Cocoa class library)
    GNUstep (see GNUstep class
      library)
+class method, 83
-class method
    isa field and, 37, 65
    NSObject class, 82
    Object class, 72
    retrieving class objects from
      instances, 65
class methods, 9, 11
    asking objects about methods
      in NSObject class, 84
      in Object class, 75

We'd like to hear your suggestions for improving our indexes. Send email to
index@oreilly.com.